HEART BREAKING OPEN
Discovering the Heart Within Heartbreak

A Spiritual Memoir

By
Lina Landess

HEART BREAKING OPEN
Copyright © 2016 by Lina Landess
Open Hearts Press
Greensboro, NC, USA

Author website:
www.linalandess.com

All rights reserved. This book or any portion thereof may not be reproduced or used in any manner whatsoever without the express written permission of the publisher except for the use of brief quotations in a book review.

Cover design by Dave Johnson, Savor Communications
Author photo by Constance Ulrich, Studio C Photography

ISBN-13: 978-0-998-09351-2
ISBN-10: 0-9980935-1-3

For my father who taught me about unconditional love, simply by being himself.

Table of Contents

Acknowledgement 9
Introduction 11
Chapter One: *On My Knees* 17
Chapter Two: *A Whole New World* 19
Chapter Three: *Hidden Wisdom* 27
Chapter Four: *Our Greatest Teachers* 41
Chapter Five: *The Great Surprise!* 47
Chapter Six: *The Gift of LovingKindness* 51
Chapter Seven: *The Challenge of Practice* 57
Chapter Eight: *Heart... Breaking... Open* 63
Chapter Nine: *The Revelation* 69
Chapter Ten: *Standing Up for Myself* 77
Chapter Eleven: *Telling the Truth* 81
Chapter Twelve: *Secrets & Lies* 85
Chapter Thirteen: *The Lies We Tell Ourselves* 97
Chapter Fourteen: *There Are No Accidents!* 105
Chapter Fifteen: *The End of the Search* 111
About the Author 123

ACKNOWLEDGEMENT

This memoir took me a number of years to write. As my spiritual journey continued to unfold and my clarity grew, I questioned myself many times as to why I was writing this book. "Who am I to write a book?" I asked—a refrain I'm sure many writers and others throughout history have asked themselves as they stepped beyond their comfort zones.

During those years, a multitude of wise teachers and loving friends have opened their hearts and their arms—as well as their ashrams, homes and retreat centers—with words of wisdom and encouragement. Included in this amazing mix of people who have blessed my life are my most beloved teachers: Swami Dayananda Saraswati (1930-2015), Jack Kornfield, a well-known treasure within Buddhist thought; A. Ramana, Elizabeth (MacDonald) Young, V. Ganesan, Linda Swanson, and Stan Davis of AHAM; my loving and loyal friends: Gene and Hardy Trolander, Charlotte and Dave Twardokus, Melinda and Jon Bern, Annette & John Davidson and, of course, Tony without whom this story wouldn't have happened. Everyone I have met, in one way or another, has served as a teacher for me. To all of them, I am exceedingly grateful.

Among those I would like to acknowledge are those who had no idea what I was up to in writing this book. They include my family; Bruce, Gloria and Kim Pfaff, my mother, Diana Baron Pfaff (1915-1996), and my father, Kenneth A. Pfaff (1917-2010).

I love you all and thank you from the bottom of my heart. Your generosity and kindness throughout has sustained me.

INTRODUCTION

Our greatest challenges often become our greatest opportunities; opportunities to discover something—a previously hidden strength, courage or wisdom within—that we otherwise might never have seen.

I'm not here to share a story of love found and lost, but rather, what we stand to discover when in the midst of those challenges we allow our heart to rule our head; when we truly listen to our own ever-present inner voice; the whisper of wisdom that lives here, inside... and trust the messages we receive.

This is fundamentally a two-fold story. It's a true tale about my personal search for meaning, and second, the realization that when the heartbreak that we fear finally happens, as it no doubt will, it carries within it the possibility of an opening—an opening of the heart that allows a deeper truth to be revealed.

As I unwittingly discovered, the heart doesn't just break... it breaks open. And within that opening lies a rich and beautiful sense of life, of love, of compassion, and what it means to be fully alive. As Leonard Cohen wrote in his song, *Anthem*, "There's a crack in everything, that's how the light gets in."

I share this story not because I think I'm special, but because there might be something here for you—a breadcrumb or two that could support and assist you with the challenges in your own life. In sharing the bare bones of my story with others over the years, I've received affirmation, again and again, that knowing about my experience could have helped them as they dealt with their own greatest challenges. While this story didn't show up in time to aid them, perhaps it can assist you now. If so, then my reason for writing will have been served.

Imbedded within my story is a concept I call choiceless choices—situations and experiences that we have no choice but to accept—no matter how strange or uncomfortable they may make us feel. It's also about how choosing fear and its accompanying ego-based choices keeps us small; in hiding from the true, happy, contented Self waiting there behind all our searching and seeking.

Over the years, I've learned the value of accepting *all* the gifts—especially those most unexpected, difficult and painful ones. It's then, and only then, when we are willing to feel fully the ache in our hearts, when we are willing to accept the pain of having our tender heart broken or our trust shaken, that we discover the grace there, behind it all. At the threshold between broken apart and broken open stands the incredible truth of our own strength and a way of being that, until that moment, we might have never known was possible.

Until that instant when my heart broke—not in the Humpty Dumpty I'll-never-be-able-to pull-myself-together-again kind of broken, but—open, I had no inkling of the richness and life-affirming power that can spring forth when we are willing to be vulnerable. There, behind the choice to stay present, to not withdraw, control or need to know what might happen next, an aliveness awaited me; a lush and vibrant fullness; a peace-fullness unlike any I had known before. And yet here it was. In my very own heart. Where, I would learn, it had always been.

As the Buddha said long ago, the suffering we undergo is the result of resisting; of trying to keep safe and avoid being hurt. We've believed for too long that keeping our hearts closed, remaining invulnerable, untouchable, protected and defended, is the only way to survive. And that's what we do. We survive. We exist. But we don't really live.

INTRODUCTION

To tell you the truth, I had never thought of writing about this experience. Then one day, out of what we've come to call the 'clear blue,' three little words; *'hearts breaking open'* tumbled into my mind. I'm not sure what I was thinking about when that phrase popped in, but I realized, as the words repeated themselves, almost like a chant, that they sounded like the title of a book—and that maybe I was being invited to write it. I've heard since that other authors have had similar experiences.

I initially thought I was being asked to write about the Buddhist practice called LovingKindness or Metta—the practice that presented itself so gracefully and powerfully when I needed it most. When it appeared, and the way it appeared, I understood that I had a choice; I could respond with Kindness to the situation in front of me or I could react. I could become a victim, one who had been wronged and betrayed and sit up proudly on my high horse. I still recall that split second when I thought about the latter choice and knew that the outcome of that reaction could only be bitterness and further hurt.

Although I didn't know what might happen if I allowed Kindness to inform my response, I did know that I was at a crossroad; that somehow, beyond my knowing, I had been changed and softened by that simple practice known as Metta. In that moment, I was being asked to simply trust my heart.

And so I chose the unknown. The untried. And with that choice, stepped into the very place I had been seeking; that place where only love, acceptance and connection live.

I've spent almost seven of the past 15 years writing this book. A few years into my writing there was an agent, one who specialized in the Buddhist market, who read my manuscript. I had received a handful of rejection letters, and had been told that a call from an agent was a rare and celebratory event. Needless to say, when she called, my heart did a flip! O.M.G. An agent. Calling. Me. She quickly nipped my excitement, gently but firmly, saying that she was calling, not to represent me, but as a courtesy to the agent of a writer-friend who had sent the manuscript to her. Although she made it clear that she wasn't going to represent me or my book, she did offer some advice.

She said that while she understood that one cannot claim to be a teacher in the Buddhist tradition unless their teacher invites them to teach, if I wanted my experience to bless others, I needed to write it from the perspective of a teacher. Her words, meant to be helpful, paralyzed me for years.

I wasn't a teacher then and I'm not a teacher now—at least not in the formal, certified, time-honored sense. I haven't been blessed by the Buddha or any of his practitioners, although Buddhist teachings have greatly influenced my life, nor has my orange-robed guru directed me to teach. I am simply a woman who has surrendered her life to seeking, and ultimately, discovering the truth; the truth that could possibly be the very same truth that Jesus meant when he said "Know thyself."

The great journey of my life has been an inner one—the search for peace and contentment; for freedom from a longing I couldn't identify, but that some wiser part of me knew had its roots in the spiritual journey. This journey is, I believe, what Mythologist Joseph Campbell called the 'hero's journey'. At the time, I thought of it as a search for meaning; a search to satisfy a deep and seemingly unquenchable thirst that I knew nothing in the world could satisfy.

As I would discover, this is a search for the Self that lies beyond any role I would play: as a woman, a daughter, a wife, a sister, an aunt, an EFT practitioner, or any of the multitude of roles we assume in our lives.

Little did I know when it began, that this would be a journey to know myself as love—the love—the Self, that simply *is*, there behind all the roles, beyond all the seeking, before all the experiences— good, bad or indifferent. This love, I know now, is the unconditional contentment that we experience when the ego—the one that convinces us that the appearance of separation and limitation are true—drops away. That love is the Truth of who I am, who you are, and what everything we observe and experience really is.

Now, with a deep sense of gratitude for the many teachers and teachings that have helped me discover that truth, it is time to share my story.

Chapter One
On My Knees

"I have been driven many times upon my knees by the overwhelming conviction that I had no where else to go. My own wisdom and that of all about me seemed insufficient for that day."
—Abraham Lincoln

Unlike our 16th president, I can honestly tell you that I have prayed—that down-on-my-knees-I-don't-know-what-else-to-do-absolute-surrender kind of prayer—exactly twice in my life. I'm not sure if that's a mark of honor or the limitation of my ego. It is fair to say that my family wasn't particularly religious. I was baptized and confirmed in the Lutheran Church, but if anyone in my nuclear family was religious, they hid it well. I hardly recall my father going to church, while my mother was sure to go on celebratory holidays like Easter or Christmas.

When I thought of prayer, I thought of religion and the dogma from which I had walked away when I was thirteen, shortly after my confirmation in the Lutheran faith. I remember the confusion I felt after being told one too many times to stop asking questions about God, and to simply believe. But I had questions; much I needed to know. It just didn't make sense. I wondered why, if God had given me a brain with which to formulate questions, I wasn't allowed to ask them. And so, I left the church.

But now, here I was—divorced from my husband, alone in a simple, second story one-bedroom, one bath apartment in Sunnyvale, California, feeling forlorn and forgotten, far from family—and the only thing I could think to do was pray. I had never felt so lost before and had no idea where else to turn. My very own, personal dark night of the soul had suddenly arrived.

I literally got down on my knees and asked for help. With knees planted firmly on the standard-apartment-quality-beige-carpet on my living room floor, I prayed. Not to God in Heaven, nor to anyone in particular, but to whomever or whatever might be out there, somewhere, to hear me. I solicited all the gods and goddesses, priestesses, and saints that might be available. I cried. I sobbed. I begged. I asked for guidance, for relief from my suffering. "I don't know what to do; I don't know where to go. I only know that I don't know. I don't know what to do next; I don't know where to turn. And I need your help. Whoever, whatever, wherever you are. Please!"

I felt cleansed at the end of my praying. I had told the truth, spoken it out loud—to myself and to any and every beneficent entity that might be 'out there' to hear me.

Do I believe there is a God? I have to say yes, but it's not the god that most churches seem to talk about. My god isn't one who looks down from a place called Heaven and decides who is deserving and who isn't. My god doesn't see Christians or Jews, Muslims or Agnostics. My God is everywhere, and everything. Although I didn't consciously know God then in the way I know Him now, I knew in my bones that God didn't have a specific address or location that kept Her separate from me or anyone else.

Chapter Two
A Whole New World

"All day I think about it, then at night I say it. Where did I come from, and what am I supposed to be doing? I have no idea. My soul is from elsewhere, I'm sure of that, and I intend to end up there."
–Rumi

Nine years earlier, as an innocent or perhaps simply naïve, newly married 23-year old from a small town in Northeast Illinois, moving to Northern California was like landing on a previously undiscovered, yet fully inhabited planet. We arrived there in the late 60's, and Northern California was abuzz. Hippies had taken over the Haight-Ashbury neighborhood of San Francisco, and the summer before our arrival had been declared the Summer of Love. My new husband and I had both grown up in Illinois and were relatively inexperienced in the ways of the world—especially the world of free love and hallucinogenic drugs. I hadn't yet smoked pot, and although I wasn't a virgin when we married, my perspective on sex was definitely monogamous. We ventured cautiously into the 'Haight' a few times, mainly to gawk at the long-haired hippies and experience the counter-culture from the comfortable distance of our car.

I had met Rob through Dave, his best friend to whom I had given my virginity. While Dave was away in the Army, Rob and I became friends. He was, as they say, 'a hunk.' As a shot-putter in the Army, his body had grown strong and well sculpted, and in his muscular embrace, I felt safe and warm. Dave and I had broken up long before my friendship with Rob blossomed into marriage... after

I balked at the requirement of Dave's Catholic faith that I sign over any children we might have to The Church.

After a cross country road trip and a brief honeymoon in Las Vegas, we arrived in San Jose, California. In my eyes, the citizens of Northern California looked different from those in land-locked Illinois. They were, for the most part, outgoing, healthy-looking, and nature loving. We found ourselves in the midst of a civilization that connected with and celebrated the natural world in a way I had never known before.

It might have been the perfect climate, or the proximity to the rocky, windswept beaches and tall, overhanging cliffs that met this part of the Pacific Ocean that created such reverence. Or maybe it was the low-slung Diablo and Santa Cruz mountain ranges that created the bowl-like valley within which San Jose and Santa Clara sit. Between these two low mountain ranges we would discover an amazing history, as well as more natural beauty than I had ever experienced growing up in the flat prairie Land of Lincoln.

But all was not ease and delight. Having worked in downtown Chicago, I'd never thought of myself as a country bumpkin, but we both found California's freeway traffic daunting. It took at least a month of stoplights and slow going on secondary streets before either of us gathered up enough courage to brave the freeway! We eventually got into the swing of things and began exploring beyond our immediate environs. Freed from our fear of fast cars and fast lanes, it was also time to look for work!

With little effort, I was hired as a secretary by one of Lockheed-Martin's subcontractors and worked in a building known as the Blue Cube; a baby blue, square, windowless, four-story edifice near Moffett Field, in Sunnyvale. The Blue Cube had been built to house the subcontractors who supported the work of the Naval Air command at Moffett. I enjoyed my co-workers, especially the young blond, blue-eyed California native who asked, when she heard that I had come from the Chicago area, if I had been in a gang! Ah, Al Capone & Jimmy Hoffa would have loved the stereotype.

Rob bounced around from job to job for a while and eventually started buying and refinishing antiques. We spent most weekends searching for old, painted, falling apart pieces of furniture in country stores, estate sales and old barns in the beautiful, Redwood-studded hills and valleys south of San Francisco. I loved the adventure as we explored back rooms and flea markets throughout Ben Lomond and Felton; small, quaint, former-logging communities nestled into the hillsides, just north of Santa Cruz.

My husband's love for and skill with reviving old wood eventually gained him a reputation as a fine, trustworthy refinisher who focused on early American oak and pine furniture. We fell in love with the warm beauty of golden oak freed from the imposition of white paint or layers of varnish and many of the pieces he transformed became part of our homes' decor. I grew to appreciate the loveliness of oak, maple, and walnut grains, as well as the rich hue of old pine. The love and care with which those old pieces had been originally fashioned became obvious as we learned more about antiques.

Unfortunately, Rob's perspective that they were marketable meant that I never knew which pieces would still be there when I came home at the end of my workday! I still remember a beautiful 36", round, golden oak table with a delicate lion's foot pedestal that he had sanded, rubbed and polished to a glorious soft satin sheen. It proudly graced our dining room—until he sold it after a year or so, without seeking my agreement. Out it went! Another piece that I grew attached to was an old, sad looking bucket style butter churn with chipped and worn white paint. I couldn't imagine what Rob was thinking when he hauled it out of an old shed in Boulder Creek. Only after he had refinished it did I realize that, like a stonemason with an ungainly hunk of stone, he was able to see the beauty hidden beneath the surface. That butter churn became a source of pride and much conversation after its rebirth as a unique oak lamp table in the living room of the sweet one-story, two-bedroom bungalow we had bought in Willow Glen, the charming older section of San Jose.

Sweetly fragrant purple wisteria flowed along the roof of the front porch and a huge old fig tree graced our postage stamp-sized back yard. Antiques filled our home, and we adopted and were adopted by Edna, the sweet white-haired widow who lived next door. It was a comfortable life. Perhaps a bit too comfortable.

Weekdays found us maintaining what might have been the routine of an old married couple living in the 'burbs. We both had steady work and in the evenings I'd prepare a meal, and after cleaning up, take our Schnoodle (Schnauzer/Poodle mix), Casey, with our two cats following along, for a walk around the block. Our elderly neighbors smiled broadly when they told me how much they enjoyed our daily little pet parade! When I returned home after our walk, we turned on the TV, and numbed our minds and our hearts in the drivel of the day. I fell asleep on the sofa more nights than I care to remember.

We had been married for about five years when Rob told me that he wanted a divorce. I was shocked, mortified, and dumbfounded. I can still remember the agony of that moment, as I sat on the floor in the hallway between our two small bedrooms, arms wrapped around my legs, head down, sobbing and wondering, "Why? What have I done wrong?" "What will become of me?" I was ashamed and afraid. Divorce wasn't a word in my vocabulary, or an idea I had entertained. Ever. I never questioned our relationship or felt that I should want more from our life together than what we had. Since Rob's parents had divorced when he was young, perhaps the idea of splitting up, of not needing a reason or making an effort to rectify what wasn't working, came more easily to him.

I didn't understand why he wanted a divorce, and we never talked about it—just as we never talked about anything important. His mind was made up and I simply, albeit tearfully, accepted it. As if I had any other option. I realized later, as happens with so many of the losses and challenges in our lives, that he had done me a favor. We weren't really happy, and we certainly weren't growing. At least not together. We were really just existing. Living a half-life.

I suppose this is what many people do. As Oscar Wilde noted long ago, we weren't alone. "To live is the rarest thing in the world. Most people exist, that is all."

If I've learned anything about life so far, these two things stand out: 1) things happen for a reason and 2) it is vital that we learn from our experiences. Borrowing from the wisdom of George Santayana, "If we don't remember (our) past, we are doomed to repeat it."

While I struggled to understand what I was meant to learn from our marriage, I recognized that it had gotten me to Northern California, where after my marriage ended, my new life would begin. Maybe that was its primary reason.

Finding a deeper meaning or purpose for that relationship has been challenging. Like so many young women of the time, my mind was filled with romantic notions about what marriage would be, yet totally unaware of the effort required to keep such a relationship fresh. From the vantage point of history, I see now that what gets lost within the fairy tale I and so many young girls grow up with is the value of friendship—of befriending your potential partner while not losing yourself, as women so often do. Being friends with another, especially one with whom there is such intimacy, requires becoming best friends with yourself first, then your partner, before you can truly commit to the highs and lows of such a relationship.

What does it mean to be a friend, a true friend to yourself? With the wisdom gained over 70+ years, I see the issue so much more clearly now. To love yourself means that you don't compromise your values or your heart so that someone else will love you. To recognize that we don't have to do anything or be anything other than who we are in order to be loved is a gift that arises out of selling ourselves short one too many times. Seeing that not being true to ourselves hasn't gotten us what we thought we wanted, we might ask, "what is there to lose by being myself?"

Loving yourself means that you can trust yourself fully. Trust your inner knowing. In Western culture, trusting our intuition has been largely discouraged. It's been put down and discredited. And yet, at the end of the day, if we learn from our so-called mistakes and missteps, we discover that there was a part of us that knew. We know, too, that if we had listened to that still, small voice that whispered so softly in our ear, we could have avoided some pain or hurt.

When we befriend ourselves we also offer ourselves the kind of love and compassion that we would naturally offer a friend. We love ourselves without judgment. That doesn't mean that we have to be perfect, but that we are willing to accept our flaws. Just as we don't need to hide who we really are with a true friend, we don't deny our shortcomings to ourselves or anyone else. My first husband and I lacked the capacity to talk, to share, to be friends enough that we could tell each other the truth. I suppose that neither of us had ever really befriended ourselves.

That willingness to be that honest, to share our fears and talk about our concerns wasn't even on our radar. Honest communication requires that we have enough trust in our lovers, our partners and our friends that we are willing to tell them our truth—and accept the outcome. Telling the truth requires us to be vulnerable.

Brene Brown, a researcher who has recently, and rightfully, come to the attention of Oprah and other media stars, wrote a wonderful book, *Daring Greatly*, about her findings regarding shame and vulnerability—and how our fear of being vulnerable so deeply limits our experience of life. Brown speaks of vulnerability this way: "I define vulnerability as uncertainty, risk and emotional exposure. With that definition in mind, let's think about love. Waking up every day and loving someone who may or may not love us back, whose safety we can't ensure, who may stay in our lives or may leave without a moment's notice, who may be loyal to the day they die or betray us tomorrow—that's vulnerability."

That willingness to take the risk to love, without knowing the outcome, is something we do naturally as children. We do it readily—until we experience the inevitable hurt. When we think that our love has been rejected, be it intentionally or accidentally, we feel as if *we* have been rejected, betrayed or abandoned. The lack of honest communication in my first marriage was, I know now, borne of neither of us realizing the importance of telling the truth about what we needed, and our fear of feeling rejected or abandoned, as we no doubt experienced as children.

Whether expressed as a heartfelt prayer to an unseen force, or the simple, honest sharing of our feelings with another, that willingness to be vulnerable, to lovingly and shamelessly tell the truth of our experience, is perhaps the greatest gift we can share— the greatest offering of love and compassion we might ever experience.

Chapter Three
Hidden Wisdom

"We shall not cease from exploration, and the end of all our exploring will be to arrive where we started and know the place for the first time."

–T. S. Eliot

Back now to that prayer; the one that took me to my knees, and changed my life.

Thankfully, one, or perhaps all, of those gods, goddesses and other unseen entities to whom I had offered my pain and longing, heard and answered that prayer. Reflecting on it now, it seems that my most desperate prayers have risen from a deep well within my being. In that well lives a sincere and absolute willingness to admit that I don't know what else to do or where else to turn.

That night, alone in my apartment, as I was swept away by an overwhelming sense of grief, I was totally vulnerable. I believed I had done everything, as taught by my culture, that I needed to do to be happy. But something was missing. I had no idea what it was; only that I felt a devastating sense of loneliness and loss—a raw and undeniable ache deep in my heart. Perhaps I had believed too much in romance, in the straight-out-of-Hollywood, saccharine sweet, everlasting notions of love and happiness that my generation had grown up on.

I don't know how prayer works for anyone else, but both of my most honest and heartfelt prayers have been answered through what I call 'middle angels;' people who show up for a split second—just long enough to point me in the direction I need to go. Without questioning, I've followed their lead and discovered the answer for which my heart longed. This was how I had led much of my life; trusting the Universe, no matter what costume the next person or guidance was wearing.

My first middle angel arrived, sans wings, in the guise of an East Indian hardware (computer) engineer. Working as a recruiter in Northern California's Silicon Valley, I focused on identifying hardware engineers for the Human Resource professionals who hired our agency. The colloquial—and I liked to tell myself loving—term for employment agency recruiters is 'headhunters.'

I was fortunate enough to be involved in the enthusiastic birth of Silicon Valley as the electronic heartland of the U.S. in the 1970's. Hewlett-Packard was ramping up; Apple Computers' Steves (Jobs and Wozniak) had only recently moved out of the garage with their personal computer, and the others—Fairchild Semiconductor, AMI, Rolm Corporation and a host of venture capitalists—were supplying the all-important electronics and funds for the growing world of computing. As headhunters, we played an important, albeit secondary, part. Engineers and scientists hopped from company to company like so many pieces on a chessboard. I loved networking within the profession and the lifestyle it afforded me. The owner of the agency I worked for set a very high ethical standard for us; as a result, the H.R. people with whom we worked respected our efforts and we were never without 'job orders.' I lived in a sweet, one bedroom apartment within three blocks of the office, and on days when a client company visit wasn't scheduled, enjoyed walking to and from work on the tree-lined neighborhood streets of aptly named Sunnyvale.

My first middle-angel was Ramesh. He was a light skinned East Indian with, as I would learn about most Indians, coconut-oiled hair that creates that lovely sheen. At the end of our interview, I asked him what he knew about meditation. He was Indian, so he would know about meditation, right? So much for assumptions. It turns out that he was born in South Africa and knew nothing about meditation. Had my search for peace already hit a dead end?

Within two weeks of our interview and my meditation question, Ramesh called to tell me that a swami would be giving a week-long lecture series at Stanford University in Palo Alto, several miles north of my apartment. In keeping with my naivete about meditation or anything about India, I asked, "What's a swami?"

Even though Ramesh told me it was simply a respectful title, used in the way Father is for a Catholic Priest, I later learned that the title swami has a much richer, deeper meaning. In Hindu culture, swami traditionally means 'Master'—one who has or is striving to gain mastery over their smaller self—their mind, or ego—so that the eternal or real Self may be recognized as the truth of ones' being.

A swami is a celibate monk or renunciate; one who has set aside all worldly pursuits to devote their life to the direct experience of the highest spiritual realization. Upon awakening to that truth, some monks may go on to teach others the truth to which they themselves have awakened.

Although often misunderstood, renunciation is neither anti-world nor based on the belief that the world is a corrupt or evil place from which to escape. Rather, renouncing the world in this way simply means that the monk or seeker has understood that there is nothing in the world that offers the permanent happiness or contentment that all humans seek. In the Hindu tradition, renunciation is the last of four stages of life, although one who feels the call to spirit may renounce and become a swami at any stage.

The preceding three stages, or ashramas, represent, in 25-year segments, the periods or phases of a person's life, reflecting both age and interest. The first 25 years are dedicated to one's education; that person is considered a student or sisya. The second quarter focuses on the worldly life, with marriage marking the end of formal education and the person assuming responsibility as a working member of society. This is the Householder or Grihastha stage. The third stage, called the Vanaprastha period, begins at the age of 50 or when the first grandchild is born. At this point, the husband (and the wife, if she chooses) begin to contemplate the deeper questions of life; Who am I? What am I here for?, etc. The fourth and last quarter of one's life is typically the time of renunciation or Sannyasa. One's spiritual study is taken up in earnest with more time spent in contemplation, often including a move to a forest ashram, totally removed from society.

As I witnessed in 2011 during my second visit to India, certain towns and cities, especially places of pilgrimage, are teeming with bearded, indigent-looking men wearing saffron-colored cloth; t-shirts, dhotis, and head scarves. On our pre-dawn walks around the Holy Hill, Mount Arunachala in Tiruvannamalai, South India, I saw dozens of orange clad men sleeping on sidewalks or the side of the road, and as the day wore on, begging for food. It was hard to know which of them were truly *sannyasins* (renunciates) and how many simply homeless.

Saffron, the color of the sannyasin's clothing, represents the fire that he or she symbolically casts his physical body into, signifying purification of the body through fire, thus freeing the soul while the body is still alive.

And so, it was into this foreign world of Hindu tradition and saffron robes that I suddenly found myself.

Ramesh and his wife met me on the Stanford campus and we sat together in a large, half-full auditorium. I had no idea what to expect. Onto the well-lit stage stepped a tall, thin man, dressed in what looked like bright orange pajamas. He sported a long, scraggly, gray and black beard, and in spite of the Halloween pumpkin-like hue of his suit, was a commanding figure. Although I was unsure of what to make of this strange looking man in his colorful attire, I found myself captivated by his words.

He spoke so clearly to my longing that I could easily have been the only person in the hall that night. This was Swami Chinmayananda, a revered speaker and intellectual from India. His life, I would discover, was the life of a true sannyasin; one dedicated to the search for truth—the very search I now somehow found myself on. He was a well-known and respected teacher of Vedanta, the revelatory philosophy of Self-Knowledge found within the Hindu scriptures known as the Vedas.

At the end of the second evening's lecture, which I eagerly attended without Ramesh and his wife, Swami Chinmayananda's spokesperson announced that morning meditations, followed by a one hour lecture would be added to the schedule beginning the very next day... at 6 a.m! I went home that night, aware that for me to make it to the meditation class by the unholy hour of 6 a.m., I would have to get up at the even more ungodly hour of 4 a.m! Although I've always been a morning person, this took the definition of morning to a whole new level. It would take something truly life-changing for me to get up at that hour!

When the alarm rang at four the next morning, a battle raged between my head and my heart. 'I'm not going,' said my head. 'Yes, you are,' responded my heart. 'No. This is nuts. (head) 'I have to go.' (heart) 'No. You don't know what you're getting into.' (head) 'True, but I have to go.' (heart)

Fortunately, my heart won that round. I went for meditation and the lecture that morning and every morning that Swamiji (the ji is added as a sign of respect when speaking directly to or about a swami) taught at Stanford. During both the morning and evening lectures his words continued to speak to my longing, to my need to know what the inner emptiness I felt was about; and to realize that there was something more to life than what I had been taught by my culture. Toward the end of the week, Swamiji's spokesperson made another announcement: Swami Chinmayanda's top student, Swami Dayananda Saraswati, also a well-known Vedanta teacher and speaker in India, would be facilitating an in-depth, 10-day Vedanta retreat at UC Santa Cruz that summer.

That was it. As clearly as I knew I had to get up for those early morning meditations, I knew I had to attend that retreat. Although I didn't know yet what I would experience during those ten days, I felt hopeful; encouraged that I had somehow stumbled onto something that might just satisfy this search for answers, for meaning, that had suddenly taken command of my life.

Several months later, I spent the better part of my two week vacation listening and learning at the feet of this teacher, Swami Dayananda, as he spoke to my heart, to my need to know that my longing could be satisfied. I understood by now that this hunger wasn't just mine, and that my search—this search for permanent, inner happiness—is something that humans have pursued throughout the ages. This journey I was now on was, perhaps, the same search that took Siddhartha, the young man who became the Buddha, to the Bodhi tree.

I was excited and comforted; I no longer felt like a misfit. I had found my tribe; others who also felt this deep hunger—who understood and shared this quest to know who we really are, and what on earth we're doing here.

That ten-day retreat with Swamiji kindled an impossibly intense need in me to know that truth for myself; to satisfy the seemingly insatiable longing for a peace and happiness I could count on. Swamiji spoke to that longing to know as an intensity; the kind of intense desire one would have to jump in a lake if their hair was on fire. What a perfect analogy! That was my condition! My hair was on fire—and the vision of Oneness held within these ancient Vedic teachings was the lake.

At the end of the retreat I found out that Radha, a young American women who had studied with Swamiji in India, would be offering classes in Vedanta and Sanskrit. Eager to keep up the momentum the retreat had awakened in me, I began attending weekly classes in Radha's small Berkeley apartment, sharing the drive with several other seekers from the south Bay. We became a band of four; three western women—a high school teacher, a secretary and a headhunter—along with a smart, young Indian fellow who worked in Silicon Valley as a software engineer.

As befits our modern day, the age-old teachings of India, as well as its customs and spicy foods, had arrived on the shores of America, and Berkeley, California—about an hour drive from my apartment in Palo Alto—was as far as we had to travel to partake of them. Berkeley had become the site for one of the first traditional South Indian restaurants in the Bay Area, and I discovered that, along with the ancient wisdom teachings of India, I loved South Indian food. My taste buds reveled in Idli—fermented rice and dal (lentils) in the form of white, spongy, slightly sour dumpling-like 'cakes'—with their spicy sidekick soup, Sambar. Masala Dosas, huge crepe-like pancakes filled with the turmeric colored tang of gently spiced potatoes and peas, overflowed the silver plates (*thalis*) on which they were served. The sourdough taste of Rava Dosa as well as the variety of chutneys, lemon pickle, mango pickle, and mint chutney tripped over my tongue like manna from heaven. I felt fully nourished—body and soul.

Six months after the retreat in Santa Cruz, Swami Dayananda agreed to teach a three-year course in the U.S., in Advaita Vedanta, the Vedic philosophy expressing the vision of non-duality. He had developed and taught this course several years earlier at Swami Chinmayananda's Sandeepany Sadhanalaya ashram in Bombay (now Mumbai), India. That first course in India was unique; Swami Dayananda had condensed twelve years of studying the Vedas, the Upanisads (*ooh-pun-e-shuds*), the Bhagavad Gita and Sanskrit with a traditional teacher (*guru*) into about three and a half years.

Perhaps most groundbreaking of all, he had allowed women (both Indian and Western) to attend that course. Based on some of the stories I've heard about that first course, allowing women into a formerly all-male program in India was not without its problems. As we have become painfully aware in recent years, India's seeming respect for their female goddesses doesn't necessarily extend to the general population of women. In a culture where there had historically been so much gender separation, young Indian men participating in the course easily fell in love with young women, Indian and American, and had a hard time understanding why their amorous overtures weren't returned.

Although I didn't know much about the content of the texts we would be studying as part of our Vedanta study, I did appreciate the context in which they would be taught. The word Vedanta literally means 'the end of the Vedas', or, 'the end of knowledge.' *Veda* or *Vidya* means knowledge and *anta* means end, so together the meaning is 'the ultimate end of knowledge.'

While the former meaning refers to the placement of the Upanisads within the Vedas, the second, deeper meaning references the truth behind all our seeking. Whereas the major portion of the Vedas focuses on the conduct of various rituals, prayers and customs meant to fulfill the human desire for material wealth and a happy life, the texts at the end of the Vedas (Vedanta) are dedicated to our ultimate search for happiness; a permanent, unwavering contentment that can never be gained through wealth, material possessions or the ever-changing conditions of life.

The wisdom reflected by this arrangement of the Vedas expresses the understanding that after all the rituals have been performed, and all the prayers for wealth and material goods have been answered, there is still a greater, more permanent kind of contentment and happiness that none of those answered prayers can ever satisfy. A quote by actor Jim Carrey says it perfectly: "I think everybody should get rich and famous and do everything they ever dreamed of so they can see that it's not the answer."

I already knew that wealth and fame weren't the answer; they are fleeting, just like the thoughts that tell us that those things, those objects or experiences 'outside' of us will satisfy our longing for contentment. As I would hear Swami Dayananda say time and again, "There is no object in the world called happiness."

As a prerequisite for acceptance into his three-year Vedanta course, we were asked to write an essay detailing why we wanted to attend, followed by a face-to-face interview with Swami Dayananda. Studying with Swamiji had now become the central focus of my life. I was a nervous wreck before and after my interview.

Arriving at his hotel room at 9 a.m. on a Saturday, I found a long line of other potential students awaiting their private interviews. As we sat outside his room, each of us lost in our own thoughts, my nerves felt as tight as a violin string. I had never actually spoken with Swamiji before and wondered if I, a still somewhat naïve young woman from Illinois, could ever be accepted as one of his students. I wondered if he had any idea how vital attending this course was to me, and how I could convey its importance during my interview. I'm sure all the others felt the same. Not knowing if I would be accepted carried its own unique sense of anguish and suffering. How unfair would it be to come this close to having *the* answers and then be denied?

The weeks following my interview dragged on interminably and I found myself unable to think of little more than becoming one of Swamiji's students. In keeping with the theory of relativity, after what seemed like months rather than weeks, the gods and goddesses smiled on me again and I was accepted as a student in Swami Dayananda's first three-year Advaita Vedanta study program in the United States! Relief and gratitude became my new companions.

Once all 45 adult students had been identified the search for the perfect place gained momentum. Radha, along with a team of supporters and students from California to Pennsylvania, began a nationwide search for a facility that was both available and affordable. We needed a property that could house us as well as serve as our school. No one knew exactly what they were looking for; just that they would know it when they found it. Just as I knew when I first heard Swami Chinmayananda.

And that was how we came to study Advaita Vedanta and Sanskrit at a former summer resort in the heart of Northern California's stunning Redwood Country... and the marijuana capitol of Humboldt County! Swamiji gave the property his blessing, citing what he said were two extremely auspicious signs; a natural waterway; the Eel River, which flowed about 150' behind the buildings, and the 90 degree bend of the river. Although the property was located 250 miles north of San Francisco, 101, the highway that linked Northern California and extreme Northern California made the ashram easily accessible to the trucks that delivered our food and other supplies, as well as the occasional visitor.

This location offered the best of both worlds; accessibility as well as a wonderful sense of remoteness. We were neither too far away for weekend visits from people living in the San Francisco Bay Area nor so close to a populated area that we would be distracted from our studies by frequent visitors or the siren call of malls and movie theaters.

Perhaps because I was already living in Northern California, I was asked to join the advance crew; a group of about eight soon-to-be students who would live on and prepare the property for the upcoming program. I wanted to make myself useful, and, truth be told, do whatever I could to help get the course started. We were busy as bees, working to transform the facility from a summer resort to a year-round, residential school.

Each of the three long, redwood-sided, flat-roofed, one-story buildings that would become our residence 'halls' held approximately twenty small, dark, redwood paneled bedrooms with small, shared bathrooms in between. Each room had a large window and a tiny closet. Given its prior use only in summer, all of the buildings had to be winterized, while the restaurant's large dining room with its huge plate glass windows overlooking the forested hills had to be converted into a lecture hall/small temple and separate dining hall. Once it was insulated, the simple wood-frame home at the south end of the property would be perfect as Swamiji's residence for the duration of the course.

The men handled the construction while the female staff set up office space in an attached section of Swamiji's house. We cleaned the restaurant kitchen from ceiling to floor and prepared hearty vegetarian meals. Living and working in such a beautiful location was simply a joy. I think we were all inspired by the mountains to our east, the Redwood groves and the Eel River to our north, and the recognition that we were helping our dream of studying with Swami Dayananda become a reality. This place would be our school and our home for the next three and a half years.

Although it took a tremendous amount of work to prepare the buildings and grounds to receive Swamiji and the rest of the students, our small band of worker bees became the heart of the student group. All of us, including most of those yet to arrive, had left our jobs and businesses for this unique opportunity to study with Swami Dayananda Saraswati.

Six months later, in November, 1979, a unique collection of 45 mostly single adults, along with several western couples and two Indian families, moved into Sandeepany West, the American version of Swami Chinmayananda's (Swami C's.) Sandeepany Sadhanalaya ashram in Mumbai (aka Bombay), India.

As I looked around at my fellow students, I had to pinch myself; I had never imagined that I would find myself in the midst of such an exceptional and diverse group of people. Ranging in age from 20 to 50, these students literally came from around the world. They had left their homes, their families and their lives in cities and countries as diverse as New York and California, Australia, Switzerland and India, each bringing their distinctive culture and life experiences with them.

We were both students and labor force, responsible for our studies as well as everything that it took to operate and maintain the ashram. A handful of 'graduates' from Swamiji's previous courses in India, from both India and the United States, acted as staff, while Radha, our former teacher in Berkeley, served as the ashram Manager. Other grads supervised and worked alongside us in the kitchen while another taught us Sanskrit so that we could follow the texts from which Swamiji taught.

Although San Francisco International airport was five hours away, Swamiji maintained a lecture tour that occasionally took him off campus and to cities across the country. While sharing the vision of Vedanta with seekers throughout the U.S., he brought in funds for our course and the running of the ashram. It was always interesting to me that when he left, when we were all looking forward to a break in the schedule, many of us would come down with some sort of illness; colds, flu, etc. It was as if the germs and viruses held off while we were busy, but took full advantage of a bit more relaxed pace!

While staff members took care of Swamiji's food, laundry and other needs, I was asked to serve as Swamiji's personal secretary and lecture coordinator. I felt blessed to have been chosen for this job and grateful that my mother had encouraged me to learn shorthand and typing. It was this skill set that allowed me to spend so much time with Swamiji and witness how deeply he cared for his followers and they for him. His written responses reflected the love and compassion of a wise and kindhearted teacher, no matter the request or inquiry he received.

That care with words was something he carried into his teaching. Setting the context for the coming three years of study, Swamiji spent our first few days of classes speaking with passion and intensity about the vital importance of language, and the language that he would use when teaching. Since Vedanta has always been conveyed as an oral tradition, he wanted to make sure that we understood the intention behind his words when teaching so that there would be no confusion on our parts. He asked us to receive the teaching with a sense of faith or trust (sraddha); e.g., with an open mind, a willingness to believe that what he said was true, unless and until we could prove otherwise.

While my dream of studying with Swamiji and having my life's deepest questions answered was being fulfilled, my parents were more than a little concerned. They were absolutely unable to comprehend my quest or the idea that I was leaving a well-paying job and a life they could relate to to study with an exotic and unknown Indian teacher. It didn't help my cause one bit that the media was obsessed with the kool-aid infused deaths of Jim Jones and the 900 members of his People's Temple, the Reverend Sun Myung Moon and his Unification Church members (known as Moonies) and their seemingly outrageous practices and mass weddings, or the reports of illicit drugs and wild sexuality at Rajneesh's ashram in Oregon. Talk about a perfect storm of reasons for parents to worry!

Some of my friends didn't understand either; one shared her fear that she might find me with long scraggly, unwashed hair and a revealing hippie dress, selling flowers, like the Moonies did, on a street corner in San Francisco.

My only choice was to listen with compassion to their concerns and assure everyone that I hadn't actually lost my mind. Since they were unable to relate to my seeking, I simply asked my parents and friends to trust me. A tall order, I know, but in my heart of hearts, I knew that Swamiji was the real deal. I was operating strictly on intuition, aware that the Universe always wants only what is best for us, and an even deeper knowing that Swamiji was someone worthy of my trust.

I realized, too, that unless a person has honestly questioned the truth of their existence, or recognized that the happiness we seek can never be satisfied through the acquisition of external objects or relationships, it is next to impossible for them to understand either the ancient inner search for meaning or those who entertain it.

What I had learned thus far about Vedanta had already allayed some of my own fears and longings, so I knew that I had no choice; this was exactly what I had prayed for. Unlike the Moonies and Jim Jones' followers, I wasn't being asked to give up my money, my family or anything else. In fact, the only financial requirement for attending the course was that every student have health insurance.

While I knew that studying Vedanta with Swamiji would change my life, I could not have foreseen the opportunities and blessings the Universe had in store for me.

Chapter Four
Our Greatest Teachers

"If you are irritated by every rub, how will you be polished?"
—Rumi

Swami Dayananda's ashram operated on the principle of Dana (donna), or generosity; a gift given from the heart. According to Hindu tradition, the society at large supports spiritual teachers and their students—much as the Kings of ancient India had. They did this because they wanted the tradition and these spiritual teachings—teachings they considered sacred and of benefit to the larger society—to always be available to all seekers. Fortunately, this custom, much like Christian tithing, continues today in many Buddhist and Hindu based centers around the world.

Because of the generosity of Swamiji's followers here in the U.S., we were able to devote our time to our studies. Just as in India, these people were devotees who valued both the teachings and our commitment, as students, to the spiritual journey. In addition to their value for maintaining the Vedic traditions, they gave with the hope that some of us would return to our home cities and share the age-old wisdom of Oneness or non-duality contained within the Vedas. And many of us did. We returned to our home cities and shared the Vedic teachings, as well as the beautiful Sanskrit language with those who had supported us but were unable to put their own lives "on hold" as we had.

Living and studying at Sandeepany West was one of the most fulfilling times of my life. That opportunity to focus on the inner search for meaning for three and one half years was a rare and special gift; and like most spiritual gifts, came with a few challenges—mostly having to do with the occasional difficult personality. For such a diverse group of people, we got along remarkably well. Perhaps because there was nowhere else to go, we had many a golden opportunity to deal with and learn from these challenges.

I recall a story that Swamiji told when the behavior of one of his graduate students provoked us. This person had some peculiar mannerisms that were particularly irritating, and Swamiji had begun receiving complaints about this Staff member from the current students.

In response, Swamiji gathered us around him during an evening Satsang (an informal time of conscious sharing between a teacher and his students) and told us a story about another teacher who was living with a group of students, one of whom was particularly difficult. (Satsang was one of my favorite times during our course; we gathered in the living room of Swamiji's house, and on cold winter nights, sat around the woodstove, listening to Swamiji's stories as he sat in his easy chair, wrapped in a handknit orange and white quilt.)

But back to the story: As a growing number of students complained to the teacher about the 'problem student,' the person in question announced that he would be leaving the ashram. When his fellow students heard this news, they breathed a sigh of relief; their nemesis would soon be gone. When word eventually trickled out that the teacher had convinced this student to stay, the other students were perplexed. "Why?" they asked their teacher. "Why are you asking him to stay? He causes us nothing but trouble." Here's what the teacher had to say, "I've asked him to stay because he is your best teacher. When you are triggered, when you have a reaction to him or his behavior, you have an opportunity to see that the problem is your reaction, not the person or situation that seemingly caused it. He is, in fact, a gift in your spiritual life."

While this was a lot easier to hear than to act on, my attitude toward *our* 'problem' staff member slowly began to transform into one of gratitude. Needless to say, this wasn't my last opportunity to let a challenging person or situation become my teacher. As long as I live, I know that this will be a critical part of my practice.

Until we see that there is really no one else 'out there;' that all the difficult people or situations we experience are only problems because of our projections, we will suffer. Things are what they are. People are who they are. Our opinions and judgments of 'others' are based solely on our inability to see with the heart, to live from the truth that what we see 'out there' is a projection of the mind—the same mind that creates that very sense of separation. That sense of separation, of duality, is the problem; a problem waiting for a solution. The solution, fortunately, is close at hand; within the realization that we are already what we seek; simple, limitless, unconditioned Awareness. The sense of duality we carry is a mind-made sense. Seeing the 'I' thought as just another thought neutralizes the power it has over us and allows us to see what is, and has always been there, behind all the thoughts.

This is the wisdom that the Vedas, the Buddha, Christ, all the wisdom teachers throughout history have shared. The desire to know this for ourselves is the foundation of the spiritual journey, through whatever means we have available.

Our days at the ashram were full, beginning with meditation at 6 a.m., followed by a morning Vedanta class with Swamiji. We attended Vedanta and Sanskrit classes in typical guru-sisya (teacher-student) style, sitting on the floor, behind short, hand-made, wooden desks. I thank my lucky stars that I was young enough then, and had a strong enough back, to withstand all those hours of sitting on the floor in a cross-legged position!

At the end of our three and a half year course of study, several of us gave ourselves a 'graduation gift' and traveled to India together—a journey that allowed us to soak in, at a visceral level, much of what we had learned about India's customs and culture during our Vedanta studies. Stories from our travels could be the topic of another book!

My return to the States after four months in India was hastened by what felt like, at times, imminent death. I, along with a handful of others, picked up a bug in Madras (now Chennai), while we were traveling with Swamiji and attending his public lectures. I suppose I had been fortunate for the better part of my time in India. I only drank water that I knew had been boiled or had gone through the charcoal filter on my portable water filtering system. With my first sip of filtered water in Chennai, I knew something was wrong. The water tasted awful! Switching to bottled water didn't help. The damage had been done and my body was soon wracked with dysentery; one of India's and other developing country's gifts to the developed world. My activities were limited to moving slowly and dizzily from my thin cot on the floor to the bathroom. Already slender, I lost a frightening amount of weight, leaving my body weaker and my mind more miserable than I had ever experienced before. Lying on that mat, feeling faint whenever I stood up, I just wanted to go home.

We had already had our visas extended an additional month after our initial three months there, and I was just beginning the process of requesting an additional months' extension when I got sick. I couldn't leave India fast enough. I had heard horror stories about Indian doctors and their unsanitary offices from Western students who had spent three years in India during Swamiji's first Vedanta course, so I refused to see a doctor there. Fortunately, one of my traveling companions had received her degree in chemistry and was able to procure medication for me at a local chemist shop. Whatever that medication was, it kept my symptoms at bay long enough to get me through the 24-hour flight back to the States.

I returned from India much worse for wear and looking little better than photos I've seen of Rwandan refugees. Although it took several months of healing, my health returned, along with my work as a headhunter in the San Francisco Bay Area. I also began teaching Advaita Vedanta to a small group of students.

Life went on this way for several years until I found myself living in another of Swami Dayananda's ashrams, this time in the Pocono Mountains of Northeastern Pennsylvania. A new crop of mostly Western students had asked Swamiji to teach another three-year course in the U.S., and Radha had asked me to serve as the Fundraising Coordinator. Since I had no fundraising experience, Radha had arranged a mentor for me; a Buddhist monk whose work as a fundraiser for spiritual entities, mostly Buddhist, put me in the mindset one needs to ask strangers and friends to donate to causes they believe in. That, coupled with my willingness to do whatever I could to make Vedanta available here in the West, took me to the Poconos and Swamiji's newest ashram.

I felt honored and blessed to help in this way and loved living in the ashram again with Swamiji and several of my *gurubhai* (family of the guru); students with whom I had lived and studied during the course in Northern California. I loved my life there, supporting this fresh group of 40 or so adult students as they studied Vedanta and Sanskrit. Being there also gave me the opportunity to attend Swamiji's Vedanta classes again. I remember feeling happier and more content than at any other time in my life.

As the ubiquitous 'they' say, timing is everything. Like so many of the events in our lives, my presence at this ashram proved to be a stepping-stone into a future I could never have foreseen.

Chapter Five
The Great Surprise!

"The greater the crisis, it seems, the greater the evolution."
–Elizabeth Gilbert

"There's no easy way to say this," he said. "I've been having an affair." It might have been shock that created the zen koan-like silence that came over me. All I know is that my husband's confession and the moments that followed served as the foundation for one of the greatest, most enlightening and grace-filled moments of my life.

This experience was the genesis of my story—the one you're reading now.

I had been living and working at Swami Dayananda's ashram in Pennsylvania as the Fundraising Coordinator for about two and a half years when Tony, my yet-to-be-recognized-second-husband showed up. I was happy with my life just as it was and felt no need or desire to change anything. I wasn't looking for a relationship, another partner, or for anything to be different in my life.

Tony and a friend of his were on their way to a ten-day Buddhist retreat at IMS, Insight Meditation Society, in Barre, Massachusetts. They had stopped at Arsha Vidya, Swamiji's ashram in the Poconos, to visit friends of theirs who were students in the current course. We met briefly during that visit and I thought no more of it, or him.

Following their Buddhist retreat, Tony wrote to Swamiji, asking if he could visit the ashram again, and stay for a month or so. As fate or karma would have it, and because Swamiji learned that Tony had some marketing experience, my wise teacher suggested that Tony and I work together to create PR (public relations) materials that could help bring more Westerners to the ashram. The rest, as they say, is history.

You might say that he charmed me. At first, I balked at the attention. As staff members we had one retreat day, or day off, a week. We could sign up for an ashram car if we wanted to go off-campus or we could simply retreat on-site. The second option, however, meant that visitors and vendors, who had no way of knowing we were on retreat, could call or stop by our rooms for ashram related assistance. If we truly wanted a day off, going off-campus was the best option.

Soon after we began working together, Tony asked if he could join me on my retreat day, sweetening the deal with the fact that he had his own car. Not wanting to seem rude, I reluctantly agreed to let him walk with me on part of the Appalachian Trail (A.T.), which had been my plan for the afternoon.

After our A.T. walk, he asked if I wanted to have dinner with him at one of the restaurants in town. I reluctantly said yes, again, and as we ate together, I picked up a vibe that made me feel very uncomfortable. He wasn't pushy or offensive in any way, but I realized that he was attracted to me; a feeling I didn't necessarily share about him.

The next morning I ran to Swamiji's room, in full panic mode, frightened by the very idea that this man might be romantically interested in me. Stream of consciousness, my fears about relationships; game playing, lies, betrayals and an entire litany of resistances flew out of my mouth. Swamiji listened patiently to my rant and at the end of it, simply said, "Tony seems like a nice fellow. Slow down... and just take it a day at a time." While this might not have been the sage advice I was seeking from my orange-robed guru, I heard what he said, and calmed down. And I took it one day at a time...

THE GREAT SURPRISE!

Tony made me laugh. Whether I laughed at his dry Irish humor or outrageous antics (one late afternoon he kept me in such stitches during a walk that he was able to steer me onto a pile of compost without my noticing until I started walking up the incline), I realized that he was a really nice guy; a guy with whom I could, and eventually did, fall in love. He was respectful, kind, funny and confident in a very appealing way. He seemed sure of himself and what he wanted from life.

I remember how, during our first passionate evening in my room, he stopped before we reached the point of no return and told me that before we became more intimate, he wanted to end his relationship with the woman he had been seeing, and that he needed to do it in person. Although this meant a trip back to Ohio for him and some time away, I appreciated his honesty, as well as his respect for her, and for me.

Ten months later, in late November, Swamiji officiated in a ceremony that combined features of both Hindu and Western weddings. Tony and I took the traditional Seven Steps (Saptapadi) around the fire together, vowing to love and care for each other forever, with about 50 of our ashram friends and two of Tony's children as our witnesses. Tony had been married before and had four grown children. Full disclosure: his first marriage ended because he was having an affair.

Following our wedding and a simple, yet joyous reception organized by our ashram friends, we drove to a charming little Bed & Breakfast in Bucks County, Pa.—our first stop on the way to Naples, Florida. After an adventurous week-long honeymoon in Naples, visiting the Everglades and biking though bird and alligator-rich areas, we left the sunny south and drove north to Barre, Mass. for my first-ever Buddhist retreat.

Chapter Six
The Gift of LovingKindness

"Like water poured from one vessel to another, metta flows freely, taking the shape of each situation without changing its essence."
–Sharon Salzberg, *LovingKindness,*
The Revolutionary Art of Happiness

Above the door of the pillared entrance at Insight Meditation Society's (IMS) Barre, Massachusetts center hangs a plaque with the word *Metta*, the Pali word for LovingKindness. I'd noticed that plaque the first time I went to IMS—during those last ten days of our honeymoon. Little did I know then the role that Metta practice would play in my journey; its gift serving as a blessing that would, ultimately, help transform my life.

Tony had suggested that we participate in a 10-day silent Vipassana (Theravadan Buddhist) meditation retreat during the last half of our honeymoon. I had never considered or experienced Buddhist meditation, and was somewhat surprised by his suggestion. It seemed strange at first, until I realized that it also felt like an affirmation; a beautiful, conscious way to celebrate and sanctify our marriage. His suggestion confirmed for me that I was marrying a man who shared my commitment to living a conscious and spiritually-based life.

I loved IMS. I also loved Jack Kornfield, one of IMS's founders and a popular Vipassana teacher. Vipassana, which means 'to see things as they really are,' is a seemingly simple meditation technique of self-observation. Thanks to Jack's Dharma talks every evening, the agony of sitting in meditation for six to eight hours every day became relatively bearable. Neither Swamiji nor Vedanta had emphasized meditation, so this practice was achingly new to my mind and my body!

As much as I appreciated the silence that was part and parcel of that 10-day retreat, I hated not being able to talk with Tony—or share his bed. We were newlyweds, after all! What were we thinking? Although we weren't able to sleep together or even talk, we did manage to slip into the forest for an occasional kiss and a little hand-holding! (Please don't tell Jack!)

In the center of the entry hall at IMS hung a bulletin board where retreat participants could post notes of an 'urgent' nature. Like teenagers urgently in love, we posted notes on the board every day, declaring our undying affection, our mutual missing, and our angst at the challenge of not looking into each other's eyes. (One of the instructions was to avoid eye contact as it is considered a distraction.)

Tony posted a note one day inviting me to meet him after lunch in the forest out behind the dining hall. He led the way as we walked, in silence, deeper into the woods. When we came to a clearing, a 6' or so circular opening surrounded by tall pine trees, he motioned for me to take off one of my gloves (it was a cold, snowy December in Massachusetts) and hold out my hand. As I did, he dropped a handful of hulled sunflower seeds into my uplifted palm, and putting his forefinger to his lips, motioned me to keep my arm up, stand still and remain silent.

Within seconds, a tiny Black-capped Chickadee dropped onto the outside edge of my extended hand, picked up a single sunflower seed in its beak and flew to a nearby tree. That bird was followed by another, and another, each waiting their turn until the one before it had flown away. I thought I would burst with excitement! What a thrill! Tony knew how much I loved birds and bird-watching. My heart still sings with the memory of how he had so lovingly planned this special encounter with my little feathered friends.

Another significant and, even more meaningful, experience took place during this retreat. Jack Kornfield, who was the main teacher for the New Years' retreat, came into the Meditation Hall each evening to sit with us and deliver a one-hour Dharma talk. Speaking one night about the importance of finding a teacher and teaching that resonates with one's soul, Jack spoke about Don Juan, the famous Yaqui teacher who taught Carlos Casteneda the Yaqui vision of reality. Paraphrasing the words Don Juan had spoken to Carlos, Jack said, *'It doesn't matter what path you take, as long as it's a path with heart.'*

I'm still not sure what it was about that string of words, but as if a laser had pierced my heart, I simply began crying. I cried and cried, giving myself over to a quiet, yet insistent torrent of tears that seemed to have been building for decades, if not lifetimes.

As my tears flowed unabated, I became aware of the other 130 or so meditators leaving the hall at the end of Jack's talk. Growing up, I had learned well the edict to not cry in public, but I honestly had no choice. The tears just poured out of their own accord. Tony gently rubbed my back and handed me tissues, staying with me as this seemingly endless river of tears emptied itself. At the end, I felt cleansed and renewed, refreshed and lighter than I had for years.

I wonder how we can carry it all—all those years and all those tears—and be unaware of them until some word or phrase, some sight or sound, calls them to the surface. Only in their absence, after they no longer existed for me, did I realize the weight of their presence. Interestingly enough, there was no emotion connected with them. They were simply tears. Released.

Two nights before the retreat ended, there was an informal gathering in the dining room. During that hour, we met and spoke with others with whom we had been sharing the intimate silence of the meditation hall. I was heartened by the handful of people who introduced themselves and thanked me for my honest outpouring of tears. They said that hearing me cry had helped them get in touch with and release some of their own long-held tears.

I have carried this lesson with me ever since. Contrary to what I was taught by my family and my culture, when we are willing to be vulnerable, to be as honest about our pain as we are our joy, we share a precious gift with others.

Through Jack's words that night I understood that even though Swamiji had a tremendously warm and generous heart, the teaching itself was dry, perhaps more intellectual than I needed. It 'worked' for me as long as I was sitting in his classes, but I didn't have a way to make what I was learning the truth of my daily experience. For me, the ancient teaching of Vedanta wasn't a path with heart.

This isn't a repudiation of the Vedas or the way Vedanta has been traditionally taught, but perhaps more about my own level of maturity. Swamiji and Vedanta represented a critical juncture on my spiritual journey, one that I will always cherish for the role it played on my path to awakening; a path that has been enriched by several teachers along the way. Swamiji, and Vedanta, were there for me as an introduction to the search for what is real; what is permanent. Their appearance in my life let me know that I wasn't crazy, and that I wasn't alone. Unlike the other 'middle angels' in my life, the ones whose presence was purposeful yet momentary, Swamiji and Vedanta have been a blessing throughout my life. All other teachers and teachings stand, as Swamiji taught, on the shoulders of those who came before; each one reflecting our growth and development as the truth of who we really are becomes clearer.

During that first IMS retreat I also learned about the heartfelt practice of Metta, or LovingKindness. As Jack shared the steps involved in this practice, I found myself deeply moved by the initial instruction—the instruction to offer love and Kindness to ourselves first. *First.* What a concept! Here was a teaching that honored the human longing, my own longing, for compassion and self-love, of self-acceptance; of the understanding that before we can truly love another, we must honor ourselves and our innate desire for health, happiness, love, and safety.

I recalled that even before my first marriage, and long before my spiritual journey began, I had had an insight, a recognition. It came to me 'out of the blue,' and I knew that it was true. I realized then that before I could truly love anyone else, I needed to love myself first. As foreign as that concept might have seemed then—given the patriarchal culture in which I grew up—I felt totally at home with it. Unfortunately, like many young women, I eventually sacrificed the wisdom of that insight at the altar of romantic love and longing.

Within Metta practice, the Buddha prescribed certain steps, the first of which, as I've mentioned, is to be kind and loving to ourselves; to wish ourselves happiness, peace, safety and prosperity. Recognizing that these qualities are what all beings want, we wish the same for others; from our friends and family to those toward whom we feel enmity or even neutrality.

Sharon Salzberg, who was instrumental in bringing this aspect of the Buddha's teaching to the West, has written several books about Metta practice. I highly recommend her books and this beautiful practice. As Sharon describes it, "Metta is the ability to embrace all parts of ourselves, as well as all parts of the world... We can open to everything with the healing force of love. When we feel love, our mind is expansive and open enough to include the entirety of life in full awareness, both its pleasures and its pains."

To benefit you, dear reader, I share here the traditional steps within this practice that it might enhance your life, as it has mine.

As Sharon states in her introduction to Metta practice, "In doing Metta practice, we gently repeat phrases that are meaningful in terms of what we wish, first for ourselves and then for others. We begin by befriending ourselves." The phrases and intentions should be authentic and meaningful to the enhancement of our lives as well as others'.

Again, from Sharon's book, the classic phrases used are:
"May I be free from danger."
"May I have mental happiness."
"May I have physical happiness."
"May I have ease of well-being."

After offering Metta to ourselves in this way, we begin extending Metta to others, starting with someone who has been very good to us, someone toward whom we feel gratitude and respect. That person, in the Buddhist tradition, is called the 'benefactor.' Next we move on to a beloved friend and/or our relatives, father, mother, sister, brother, and so on, to include animals and pets. From here we offer Metta to someone with whom we might have difficulty, allowing our hearts to open to all matter of beings in the world.

Our next offering of Metta is to someone toward whom we feel neutral. They are neither friend nor foe; someone about whom we feel neither animosity nor friendship.

From this neutral person things become more challenging. We next offer Metta to someone with whom we have experienced conflict—a person we fear or toward whom we have anger or an inability to forgive. The Buddhist scriptures consider this person 'the enemy.' This step of the process invites us to experience our capacity to step out of our ego-mind—the mind of separation—and shift from conditional to unconditional love. Sharon puts it this way: "Here we learn that the inherent happiness of love is not compromised by likes and dislikes, and thus, like the sun, it can shine on everything. This love is truly boundless. It is born out of freedom, and it is offered freely."

Chapter Seven

The Challenge of Practice

"May we be strengthened with the understanding that being blessed does not mean that we shall always be spared all the disappointments and difficulties of life."

–Heber J. Grant

Despite the rigor of meditating for ten hours a day for ten days straight, being on retreat was, in many ways, the easy part. In the company of others, with the discipline of set times for sitting and walking meditation and no other responsibilities, showing up for practice simply happened. Maintaining a practice in the midst of our busy daily lives proved to be a much greater challenge.

We'd been married for about four years when we bought a 70's ranch-style house on one and a half acres of land on the outskirts of the village where Tony lived before we met. Although the house was dark, dirty, and needed a mountain of work, Tony somehow saw its potential. Because he didn't normally or happily spend his hard earned money, I was surprised when my husband told the realtor we would buy it.

Tony acted as the subcontractor, ably transferring the ideas in our heads onto sketchpads for our construction crew. I discovered, and was impressed by, his skill as an artist and thought it sad that his family, like so many others of his parents' generation, had convinced him to abandon his talent and passion as an artist and take up a more financially lucrative, business oriented practice. Having said that, I also appreciated that because of his work in the world, we were able to buy this house outright.

We worked well together throughout the process, sharing our ideas and visions of how we wanted to transform this cold, rambling, uninspiring three bedroom, two bath house into a comfortable, light, warm and welcoming home. The renovation began when Tony and I enthusiastically took a sledgehammer and crowbar to the wall that separated two of the small, dark bedrooms. This new, larger room would soon become our light-filled master, en suite.

Our construction crew handled the rest, replacing small rectangular windows on the long side-wall of our bedroom with larger, more modern ones. They tore out the rear wall—the one that overlooked the back yard and our future Japanese garden—and installed French doors. The impact of these relatively simple changes was remarkable; we had begun the process of opening the space and inviting the light outside in.

I've always loved the idea of window seats; cozy, warm spaces in which to relax with a book or take a little nap. Working with our construction crew, Tony designed a lovely window seat nestled between our new 'his and her' corner closets. With his artist's perspective, he introduced other features that reflected both our interests and his creativity.

In the style of 70's ranch houses, all the rooms were separated by walls. The kitchen was a mash-up of walls, doors and doorways; one opening led into the dining room, another into the hallway leading to the living room and bedrooms, and a third doorway led into a small pantry and the door to the back patio. As part of the process of opening up the kitchen, we were thrilled to continue deconstructing.

We removed the walls separating the kitchen from the dining room and the living room, as well as the wall that created the pantry. Because we had removed all these walls, we needed to find a place for the refrigerator. The only possible location for it now was in front of the opening into the hallway—not an aesthetically pleasing choice.

Tony came up with a solution that I absolutely loved. With the back of the fridge facing the 'former opening', he envisioned a wall with glass shelving for books and art objects. Our builders closed in the kitchen side of the opening, and Tony lit the new glass shelves from underneath with a simple picture light. This sweet space not only solved the dilemma of that extra doorway, but lent the house and the hallway one more special touch; a fitting location to display some of our favorite books and smaller art pieces.

When we replaced the dark, dirty rust-colored carpet that ran throughout the house with a beautiful off-white berber, everything came together in ways that we hadn't imagined. I remember the two of us standing there after the carpeting was installed, stunned by the rich quality of light that the carpet added. This was, indeed, the pie'ce de re'sistance... the transformation of our home was now complete!

Our relationship survived not only the stress of remodeling, but living there while the hammering, sawing and painting went on around us. While the front half—the living room, kitchen and dining room—was being remodeled, we lived in the back half; our bedroom, bath and second bedroom/office area—and visa versa.

As we shifted clothing, shoes and bedding from one end of the house to the other, and basically camped in a 300-400 foot construction-free zone for what felt at times like an eternity, we retained a relatively good sense of humor. I credit our shared Buddhist practice and our commitment to LovingKindness for this. Had these practices not been a foundational part of our life, I don't know if we would have made it through all the dust and deconstruction!

Shortly after the remodel was complete, we began sitting daily for about an hour each morning. So committed were we to a daily practice that we had a dedicated area in our bedroom; a small but cozy space where our zabutons and zafus sat, overlooking the soon-to-be-created Japanese garden that Tony would spend painstaking hours designing. He poured over Japanese garden books, moved, I imagined by his desire, as an artist, to create a 3-D work of art; one through which we could walk, sit and perhaps re-experience the serenity and peace we had found during our annual Buddhist retreats.

I thought the strength of our relationship had been tested and proven even before our marriage, during a month-long cross-country car-camping trip from Pennsylvania to California. Although neither of us had been camping beyond our adolescent scout-related outings, we were up for the adventure as part of a 'where would we like to live?' discovery tour.

We had a blast on that trip! After leaving Swamiji's ashram in Pennsylvania, we drove north to Hartford, Connecticut, west to Boulder, Colorado, south into the stunning landscapes of Southern Utah and New Mexico, camping and hiking through the sun-kissed lands that house the wind-swept formations of Bryce Canyon and the awesome red-rock cliffs of Zion National Park. Along the way, with the intention of checking out a variety of potential places to live, we stopped in cities and towns where one of us had a friend or two nearby. While scouting for the right place to live, we were able to use our cross-country journey as an opportunity to both reconnect with and introduce our new partner to dear old friends.

Arriving at the home of a friend in Northern California, I was thrilled to share some of my favorite places with Tony. We traveled along the magnificent Pacific Coast Highway, visited Big Sur and stayed for a few splendid days at the Esalen Institute, basking in a hot tub while overlooking the Pacific Ocean. When we stayed in Santa Cruz with friends of mine before heading back east, I witnessed Tony's shocked response to his first earthquake as the ground shook and the quintessential chandelier swayed over our heads at the dining room table.

Our moods were light and carefree when we returned to Wellspring, Ohio, where we stayed with one of Tony's friends. We spent weeks weighing the pros and cons of each city and town we had visited, and after much debate, agreed that this funky, welcoming little community, where Tony had been living before coming to the ashram, seemed the most sensible, both in terms of his work and our ability to afford a home.

Chapter Eight
Heart... Breaking... Open

"Before you send the heartbreak away, turn into it and open. It is bestowing a transmission of pure revelation, but it is not easy to receive. Hold the offering close and see if your heart truly wishes to be mended. This raw, tender, broken openness is your lifeline to intimacy with all things. Offer safe passage for your vulnerability, for this is your gift to a world that has forgotten."

–Matt Licata

I fell in love with Wellspring and found myself readily absorbed into village life, perhaps more so than Tony ever had. This was, and still is, the kind of community that not only values, but encourages citizen participation; an invitation the majority of its residents take seriously.

I became involved in community events and created a few of my own as the spiritual journey drew me to the Divine Feminine of ages past. I found comfort in the discovery of ancient Greek goddesses and how their characteristics—the qualities by which they were identified—are relevant to the lives of modern women. As my knowledge and excitement about the ancient Goddesses grew, I began offering workshops for other women who, like me, had no prior knowledge of them. During these workshops, I shared my understanding and enthusiasm about how recognizing the qualities of these ancient Goddesses—their spirits, their strengths, and what they stood for—could inform and transform our lives.

By now many people have heard about a number of these Goddesses, such as Artemis, Athena, Aphrodite, Demeter and Persephone, as information about them has made its way into mainstream culture. Women today, aware of how we have lost so much of ourselves living in purely patriarchal cultures, have begun to embrace the Divine Feminine as a source of strength and inspiration. We intuitively know that without the return of the feminine into our world we are doomed to live lives of repression and disrespect, of war and destruction of all that we hold dear, including our precious Mother, Earth.

As Dianne Laramee, a personal researcher and development coach says, "The understanding that results when we intuitively or intellectually grasp the meaning of the gods and goddesses myths can be both powerful and healing. By knowing who our god/goddess archetypes are, we can be aware of the potential within us that is a source of spirituality, wisdom and action. Sometimes we need to hear the voices. We listen to them in the voice of others and in the quiet spaces of our meditations.

We listen for voices that we can draw on for guidance

Voices that support us in making choices that reflect the god/goddess within

Voices of creativity, personal integration and joy."

I also discovered Buddhist practitioners living and practicing in this community. Along with churches representing almost all the faith groups, several Buddhist practitioners had created a small Dharma center where all three schools of Buddhist practice—Theravadan, Vajrayana and Mahayana—were honored. Each tradition had its own scheduled days and times for practitioners to come together to practice their particular form of Buddhist meditation. I became a regular participant in the Sunday morning Vipassana meditation group and valued the deep sense of community that grew out of the silence we shared.

Meditating on the cushion in the silence of a retreat or Dharma Center is one thing. That night on the white loveseat, back in our living room, I was invited to take my meditation practice off the cushion and into my life. This is, of course, the definitive test... and one of the reasons we meditate.

Tony's confession about his affair offered me the ultimate in what I call choiceless choices. Just as I had had no choice when suffering first set me on the spiritual journey, the only real choice I had now was to surrender to this situation. Nothing I could have said or done would change the circumstances. Tony was having an affair. This was the truth; his truth. And now it was mine.

That evening, as I looked into my husband's weary, hazel eyes, these words—expressing a sentiment so unique that I still remember them clearly—simply fell from my mouth, unexpected and unrehearsed. As if a wiser, more compassionate and loving part of me had taken over, I simply said to him, in a sure, confident, calm voice: *I can't imagine that we'll ever have a better opportunity than this to practice LovingKindness.*

Without a moment's hesitation, he agreed, and we spent the next two and a half hours calmly talking about the possibilities before us. We agreed that we now had a chance to transform our marriage—and our lives. He reminded me, as we spoke about the possibilities, that the Chinese symbol for crisis also means opportunity. And so, from this very personal crisis we acknowledged that we now had a very personal opportunity; an opportunity to look at what was working, what wasn't, what had brought us to this crossroad, and to explore how or whether we would move into the future as a couple.

We had been married for about seven years when he told me he had betrayed us. I say *us* because our relationship was an entity; one that we had unknowingly created when we married. I remember attending a couples' workshop facilitated by a therapist friend of Tony's. During the workshop, he invited us to consider that the relationship formed when two people come together in marriage is an entity in and of itself. With this philosophy as its foundation, marriage has the potential to become less about each individual and more about how to fulfill their commitment to the relationship; something greater than either individual. In the fulfillment of the relationship, both partners would also, ultimately, feel fulfilled.

Thinking about this now, I recall that Swami Dayananda spoke of marriage as a pact wherein each partner is committed to making the other happy. If making your partner happy, he said, is the most important goal in your relationship, then both partners end up happy and the marriage will be a success.

Although we both forgot that holistic perspective immediately after the workshop, our relationship was often incredibly beautiful. We had shared some deeply tender times; times when we loved each other more fervently than I had known was possible.

Was his affair the seven-year itch people talk about? Would this pass as a dalliance, a brief interlude that had little meaning? I didn't consider those possibilities then; I only knew that I loved this man more than I had ever thought possible.

How do couples express the depth of their love? While I know that it must differ for everyone, one example that stands out for me happened one beautiful Fall afternoon. We'd been out in our back yard, raking the leaves that had fallen from the tall oak and elm trees that marked the periphery of our 1.5 acres. We were in high spirits, laughing and whooping as we jumped into leaf piles like a couple of kids. Later, back inside the house, we sat in our dining room, aglow in the love that, like a small forest stream, meandered quietly and gently between us.

I'm not really sure how it came up, but we simply began talking about having a child. As corny as it sounds to me now, we imagined our 'love child;' a little being who would reflect the love now flowing between and around us. I sat on his lap as we pondered the possibility, feeling closer to him than I ever would again.

I was in my mid-40's then, and he was 14 years older. As wondrous as our love-child fantasy felt, our conversation eventually grew more practical and as it did, we agreed that it wouldn't be fair for a child to have such ancient parents; when he or she was a teenager, Tony would be 80 and I'd be in my mid 60's. The inspiration within that tender, loving moment fell gently away.

And now, not so many years later, here we were—having a very different conversation.

Chapter Nine
The Revelation

"Sometimes the best and worst times of your life can coincide. It is a talent of the soul to discover the joy in pain—thinking of moments you long for, and knowing you'll never have them again. The beautiful ghosts of our past haunt us, and yet we still can't decide if the pain they caused us outweighs the tender moments when they touched our soul. This is the irony of love."

–Shannon L. Alder

"We have to talk," he said, as he stepped over the wide oak threshold that separated the tiled entryway from our living room and moved rapidly toward the off-white loveseat against the far wall. Having seen the headlights of his car coming up our driveway, I had just set the table for his dinner. I followed him into the living room, aware of a sense of foreboding akin to that of a student called into the principal's office. I sat kitty korner from him at the L-shaped junction our loveseats formed, and waited, curious to know what was so pressing.

And then, that statement; the one I may never forget, "There's no easy way to say this. I've been having an affair."

Words failed me. I was silent. After a moment, I calmly asked if I knew 'her.' "Yes," he said. It was Lara; a slim, long-haired, freckle-faced blond whom I had met in India more than a decade before meeting Tony. She was now a yoga teacher, living nearby with her husband and their little daughter. Irony aside, I had introduced her to Tony when we ran into each other in town one day. A month or so later, she invited us to dinner at her home. We shared a meal, laughter and a sing-along with her guitar-playing husband, and some time later, she had become a client of my family therapist husband.

I questioned him, then, curious as to how long their affair had been going on. His answer was vague. "A number of months," he said. Next, I asked, "Why are you telling me now?" "Because," he said, "I didn't want you to hear it from anyone else."

In the next moment, I was out of the room—not physically, but in what I could only later presume was a mystical experience. Although I had been on the spiritual journey; seeking peace of mind and freedom from the all-too-human sense of limitation for 15 years by then, mind-altering psychedelics and alternative states of consciousness had never been part of my practice.

And yet, without moving from my seat, I suddenly found myself in what felt like a dimly lit cave. As my eyes adjusted to the low light, I saw a glistening black object rising and falling, carried along by dark, moving waves. Was it a log? A raft? No... it looked like a sleek, shiny, black otter! As I watched, she twisted and spun, her body undulating within the forward motion of a small, yet fast flowing, underground river. I have no idea how long I stood there; it could have been two minutes, or two hours. Entranced, I simply watched this beautiful creature rise and fall, dancing and cavorting through the waves as they carried her along. And then it was over. She was gone. There was no sound, no clear message; only the memory of this sleek, black, dancing otter.

As the otter and her cave disappeared, I heard a man's deep, resonant voice, recounting a story about the Dalai Lama and his expression of Kindness. I had heard this story several months earlier, during a week-long Vipassana meditation retreat at Grailville, a simple, yet charming retreat center south of Cincinnati. Anna

THE REVELATION

Douglas, a well-known and inspiring Vipassana teacher from the San Francisco Bay Area, had shared it with us during that retreat.

According to the story, the Dalai Lama was overseeing a celebration at his home in exile in Dharamsala, in the Himalayan Mountains of northwestern India. As is typical of most Tibetan festivities, monks in maroon and yellow robes were chanting their deep-throated, resonant chants. There was music and drumming, and the smell of incense filled the mountain air. As the story goes, a bicycle messenger rode up the hill, and dropping his bike on the ground, rushed to the dais on which His Holiness, the Dalai Lama sat. His Holiness received the telegram from the messenger and as he stood up, a hush fell over the crowd. After silently reading the telegram, the Dalai Lama spoke to those gathered around him, "I have received news that fourteen of our nuns and monks have been tortured and killed by the Chinese." Pausing briefly, he continued, "Let us pray for our nuns and monks." Pausing once more, he said, "And let us pray for the Chinese."

Coming to me as it did then, in the privacy of my own mind, I understood that I had a choice; I was being invited to *respond* to my husbands' news rather than react. To be a woman who had grown and matured; one who could, in her deepest, darkest moment, call on the teachings she had received, and allow them to bless her. It was Kindness that called to me then. This practice known as Metta—the practice I had learned years before while on my first silent Buddhist retreat and had made a regular part of my life—stood before me now. Mine to choose.

How much clearer could a message be? From the Dalai Lama and the element of water to that incredible otter, I recognized that I was receiving a blessing and an amazing invitation! I was, in essence, being guided and summoned to meet this situation from an open, kinder and gentler perspective; a perspective that carried with it symbology that called up even deeper meanings; symbology whose meanings were not wasted on me.

According to Native American culture, Otter, as an animal totem or symbol, is an expression of the feminine principal. Mypoweranimal.org says this about otter: "Otters represent the feminine aspects of creation, imagination, joy and love. Otters glide through the emotional difficulties of life effortlessly and can teach us how to do the same. They know how to float on the currents of life enjoying the beauty that it holds."

Beautifulspiritualsouls.com says this about water: "Spiritually speaking, the element of Water symbolizes our emotions that ebb and flow. Water teaches us control over that cycle as well as reminding us that change is inevitable. When an idea forms, water initiates action. It liberates our steps while never being far from the heartbeat of the world, or each living thing."

In the Taoist tradition, water is considered an aspect of wisdom. "The concept here is that water takes on the form in which it is held and moves in the path of least resistance; the symbolic meaning of water speaks of a higher wisdom to which we may all aspire." (Whats-your-sign.com)

Even without the benefit of those perspectives at the time, I understood that the only choice I had now was to honor the vision of Otter, to step into what the Dalai Lama had taught, and meet my husband's confession with a kindness and wisdom that arose, naturally, from my suddenly broken, yet open, heart.

In spite of our honest and hopeful sharing following his confession, and the inclusion of LovingKindness into the situation, at the end of our conversation, I felt raw. Undone. Heartsick. I would sleep alone that night in our bed. I told him, my voice shaking, that I just couldn't share our bed with him. He didn't argue, aware perhaps, of how violated and betrayed I felt. My heart was bruised, wounded. He had suddenly become a stranger to me. A man I didn't really know. He made up a bed of blankets on the floor of his home office, next to our bedroom. The next morning there was nothing more for us to say. We didn't speak or look at each other. My heart felt numb. Shattered.

At work later that morning, when I answered the office phone, I heard the voice of Will, Lara's husband. "I think your husband and my wife are having an affair," he said. He had seen them the day before. In Tony's car. In a place they shouldn't have been. Together. It turns out that he was the 'anyone else' Tony didn't want me to hear the news from.

With a sinking heart, I told him, "I know. Tony told me about it last night." Will was angry. No, not angry—he was filled with rage. Pain. I tried to comfort and calm him, to let him know that I shared his hurt. I suggested that it would be important for us to understand what had gone so wrong in our marriages and not simply point fingers. Why had our partners sought each other out? When we hung up he seemed calmer, a little less angry. I was shaking.

Walking through town later that day, I felt like a stranger in a familiar, yet suddenly foreign landscape. Acutely aware of my footfalls on the sidewalk, I had what I can only imagine might be the experience of a sleep-walker stepping into the wakeful world. I carried a secret now; something that no one could have guessed by simply looking at me. No matter how I saw myself before, I was no longer her. I felt alien, awkward. In a strange and disconcerting way, I no longer knew who I was.

I spent the next several nights at the home of friends, safe and warm in their kindness. I felt betrayed, and my heart ached so, that I couldn't imagine sharing our home, let alone our bed with Tony again. I wanted to hurt him, to make him worry about me—the way I had worried about him on those late nights when he was supposedly 'working.' Even though I had been the one to suggest LovingKindness as our touchstone, part of me wanted to make him suffer. That all too human hurting part of me didn't want to let him off so easily.

After much soul searching and conversation with my friends the next morning, I realized that my commitment to LovingKindness was greater than my desire to create more suffering. Even for Tony. Just as I wanted happiness and peace for myself, in my heart I wanted happiness and peace for him as well. His voice was gentle when we spoke, filled with both sadness and gratitude for my call.

Although I felt deeply wounded, I didn't hate Tony. I realized that even as he had betrayed me, I had, long before, betrayed myself. Why do I say that? I have learned over the years that the world 'outside' of us is merely a reflection of the world inside of us; inside our minds, an expression of our thoughts. Betrayal or any other experience is, in truth, simply a projection; a manifestation of our beliefs; expressions of our greatest and worst fears and triumphs. The Buddha said it this way: *"We are what we think. All that we are arises with our thoughts. With our thoughts, we make the world."*

My self-betrayal arrived in the form of fear; fear that if I told Tony about my unhappiness in our marriage, my wish that he could be more present, more available, to fill my days and nights with the kind of love and tenderness we had shared in earlier times, that he might reject me.

I know now that I wasn't alone with that kind of fear. Many of us, especially women, keep our feelings to ourselves for fear of being left on our own; for fear of losing the security we have, even though we are unhappy or physically or emotionally abused by our partner. I was conscious of the role I had chosen in our personal drama and that the only honest thing I could do was take responsibility for it.

I knew, too, that I had in some way brought this upon myself. I had even wondered, from time to time, what I might do if a husband of mine, not this one in particular, but anyone to whom I was married ever had an affair. Now I knew.

I returned home after several days and we tried to communicate from a heartfelt place. It felt forced. Sharing space with him was awkward. We felt like strangers; people who were suddenly unsure of each other. Our bond; the bond I thought we shared, had been broken; I had no idea if or how it could ever be repaired. We resumed our work routines, and made an effort to continue a 'normal' life together. In spite of my spoken commitment to LovingKindness, keeping my heart open to him was often a challenge. This situation required more of me, at times, than I was capable of delivering.

I eventually moved out of our home and into a friends' sublet, closer to town. The singular motivation for my move was to get away from the ongoing betrayal. The hang-ups—times I answered the phone only to have the caller hang up—got to me. Coming home from work only to see Tony hastily hang up the phone became like a scene from a B-movie. Although my brain may not be as advanced as that of a rocket scientist, it didn't require an exceedingly high level of education or insight for me to realize that, despite my pleas that he stop communicating with or seeing her, 'she' was still very much in his life. And mine.

After I moved out, Tony maintained contact. We talked once or twice each week, and after a couple of weeks, he suggested a unique arrangement. He said that he felt bad that I had been the one to move out—and that I shouldn't be the only one inconvenienced. His idea was that while one of us lived in the house for a week, the other could stay elsewhere; we could share our home, just not at the same time. While I appreciated his idea, moving every week seemed disruptive. We agreed that three weeks at a time was a bit more reasonable and lived out this arrangement for several months.

Before learning about Tony's affair, I had been seeing an amazing therapist, a wonderfully skilled woman who was helping me address both current and family of origin issues. In spite of Tony's initial reluctance and conviction that as a therapist himself he knew "all the tricks," he agreed to meet with my therapist and possibly enter into couples' counseling. Impressed after meeting her, he agreed to participate with the goal of seeing if our marriage was salvageable.

As we entered this new phase of looking deeply into what had gone so wrong in our relationship, I asked him for just one thing; that he stop seeing Lara.

While he never outwardly refused my request, neither did he honor it. Like Damocles' sword, my request simply hung in the air.

Chapter Ten
Standing Up for Myself

"Be content with what you have; rejoice in the way things are. When you realize there is nothing lacking, the whole world belongs to you."
–Lao Tzu

I wish I could tell you that LovingKindness was my steady companion; that my every thought and word was loving and kind. Although I kept up my daily meditation and LovingKindness practices, our fractured relationship served as a constant test of my spiritual maturity.

One day I totally failed. I can no longer recall the details or why we were at the house at the same time. Perhaps we were making an effort to talk outside the therapist's office or because our 'home stays' overlapped, but there we were. Somehow he let it slip that she, his lover, had been there. At our home!

I imagine that the fire shooting from my eyes startled him. Although he tried to calm me down with the assurance that she hadn't actually been *in* the house, but only in the garden, I was inconsolable. I was outraged and outrageous, like a mother bear defending her cubs. The garden, *our* garden was a space as sacred to me as anything within our home's four walls. We had worked together, designing, discussing, and bestowing as much loving attention on the creation of our peaceful Japanese garden and the surrounding land as we had the house. And he had brought her *here*! Yet one more betrayal!

"Now," I screamed, "not even the ground around me is free of her!" Everything I cared about had been ripped away and he just kept tearing! LovingKindness took not just a backseat, but totally disappeared from my radar. No thought of Kindness touched my mind. I screamed. I raged. I finally let him have it. No more Kindness, no more compassion, no more heartfelt effort. I simply didn't care.

I needed to do this. I had to let him know that I would no longer roll over and simply accept the decisions he made with respect to his lover. I wanted him to care about me—about *my* feelings! Maybe I just wasn't that enlightened, after all. In that moment it didn't matter. And I didn't beat myself up about it. Instead, I felt vindicated, clear, washed clean. Tony had never seen me like this. Nor had I.

It felt good to speak up for myself and say what I really felt. Finally. Maybe I had held my feelings in for way too long. I hadn't told the truth about my loneliness and unhappiness in our marriage—for fear of losing what I thought I had. Now with nothing more to lose, I simply let my anger; this hot, seething volcano erupt. We had never fought like this. We had argued, had normal disagreements, but we were much too civilized to shout.

Having grown up with a mother who yelled a lot, I had made a commitment to myself, long before my first marriage, that I would never lose my temper and yell at anyone. Laughable now, I remember shouting once at my first husband during an argument. As soon as I realized that I was yelling at him, I began to cry. I had, in that instant, broken my vow to myself and become my mother! He was as shocked by my tears as I was by my fury. Moved by my tearful admission that I had just become my mother, he laughed, gave me a hug, and we made up then and there.

Now there was no tear-filled upset. No frightened apology. No remorse. I felt my power. Born on the cusp of Cancer and Leo, I let my lion roar!

STANDING UP FOR MYSELF

It was almost as if his affair had unleashed something in me that had lain dormant for far too long and it was time for me to stand up for myself and tell the ragged truth. I kept my cool as long as I could… until that was no longer an option. At times it felt as if he was goading, almost encouraging me to rage. How would you feel if your spouse told you that he/she loved someone else and wanted to marry them? "Have you forgotten that you're already married?" I screamed. We were, of course, having another fight. The kind of outrageous reaction to each other that we had never had before. Any loving feelings between us now lay shattered in the wake of the drama unfolding before us. Between us. He was more concerned about what would happen to him, to his career as a therapist than the state of our relationship. He paced back and forth in the living room, in utter terror that he might lose his license to practice. As if I should care, he shared his fright and fear with me. All I could do was listen and witness his undoing. I just stood there. He had brought this upon himself but wanted my compassion. I simply couldn't give it.

In spite of my temporary lapse of Kindness, I didn't give up, nor did I admonish myself. Whether at home or my friends' sublet, I continued my daily hour of meditation practice along with 10 minutes of LovingKindness. My meditation bench became my anchor; the one thing I could count on, every morning, no matter what else might be going on in my newly chaotic life.

Meditation strengthened and deepened me; allowing moments of calm in the midst of the storm swirling around me. I recall one morning, one ordinary moment, when I was staying in our home. I was simply walking through the living room toward Tony's low-slung, cedar credenza where we kept the stereo. Mid-step, I became aware of my foot moving slowly through space. In that moment, my mind fell utterly still. I became the witness. There was only this foot. Moving. Silently. Through space. Stillness surrounded me. Beingness. Peace. Just. This.

Although I might use different words now to describe that experience, as soon as the moment had passed, I understood that I had just experienced 'Beginner's Mind'—the term Buddhists use to describe that pure state of openness and curiosity, a mind-space free of concepts and conditions. What we now call 'Presence.'

That moment was a beginning. An affirmation. A seeing into Truth. And although Buddhist practice was my reference point then, I now see Beginner's Mind, that point of seeing, of simply Being, as simple Awareness. The Awareness that is always there, always here, present, behind the phenomena we call the world.

That seeing, that experience of simple Beingness, became a touchstone for me. A glimpse into that which would carry me further and deeper on my spiritual journey.

Chapter Eleven
Telling the Truth

"Do not assume that divine guidance flows only when you are in need of help. Guidance continues to flow whether or not you have problems. It transcends problems, heartbreaks, and traumas, flowing through dreams and illuminations. Whether guidance comes during times of tranquility or trauma, however, it is up to you to have the courage to acknowledge it."

–Caroline Myss

Tony and I continued the creative sharing of our home as well as weekly sessions in my therapist's office. Six months into our couple's counseling, I asked him once again for the only thing that I had been requesting all along; that he cease all contact with Lara, at least long enough to give our relationship a chance.

This time, rather than say nothing as he had before, he flatly refused. At the end of the hour, as he and Jasmine were checking their calendars to schedule our next session, I told them not to bother. They looked at me, unsure of what I was saying. But to him, I said, "If you won't stop seeing your girlfriend," I said, "I see no reason why we should continue. There are three of us in this relationship and as long as that's so and she's not in this room, I see no purpose in maintaining this farce. I'm done."

I had been patient long enough. Although I hadn't planned to end our counseling sessions, it seemed like the only option I had left.

It was time to speak up for myself. I had done enough, tried enough and was just plain tired of living this way; of playing this game. His game. I was ready to end the charade and move on. Perhaps because it came to me in the moment, without rehearsal, I wasn't afraid.

My old friend, fear, had left the room and truth had made me stronger.

I felt no anger or remorse. There was no second-guessing whether I had done the right thing. I had told my truth and stopped the pretense that we were making any progress.

I had simply surrendered to the truth of the situation. Again. While I seemingly had no power over what was happening, by simply accepting the facts as they were, I found harmony within myself; the only place harmony can truly ever live.

With that simple act of acceptance, I reclaimed not only my self-esteem, but the peace that is there at the end of all conflict. I couldn't do anything that would change the situation, so I simply changed my mind.

As much as I had hoped that we could mend our broken relationship, I had once again come to terms with reality. As that old adage reminds us, it takes two.

Reluctant as I am to admit it, this was the first time in my life that I had been willing to stay in a relationship, and try to work things out. I hoped that we might be able not just to salvage our marriage, but to see how we, and our relationship, could grow stronger as we healed our personal and shared wounds. I hoped that we would stay together and discover what it means to support each others' spiritual growth; what my therapist had told me was the true purpose of marriage. But that was not to be.

After ending our couple's therapy and acknowledging that our marriage was undeniably over, we began dividing our material goods. We agreed again to use LovingKindness as our foundation. As a result, we argued very little and let practicality guide the majority of our decisions. Tony had brought several beautiful pieces of antique furniture—a tall pine corner cabinet, dark walnut dressers and a few other large items—as well as some beautiful artwork into our relationship and had, years earlier, asked me to make sure, if he died before I did, that his children would receive them as part of his estate. As much as I loved those pieces, they were clearly his. Since he didn't care to cook, I took most of the small kitchen appliances; the food processor, the blender, good knives, dishes and cookware, while we divided the furniture and artwork that we had bought together.

Shortly after this relatively congenial parsing out of our material possessions, we appeared before a civil court judge to have our divorce granted. When the judge asked if we were sure about divorcing, against the truth pounding in my heart, I followed Tony's lead and said, "Yes." Now it was done.

Since Tony had funded the down payment on our home, he remained there and I moved into town, with his assurance that if and when he sold the house, I would receive half the proceeds. I lived in a small well-lit basement apartment where I devoted two years to writing the first draft of this book. Many times during those years we got together to resolve questions that had arisen mainly for me with respect to things that had happened during our marriage. Tony was always willing to meet with me as we shared insights and realizations about those experiences and to take responsibility for our shortcomings.

We gradually and honestly settled our unfinished relationship business through these conversations and, after several years of what felt like half-hearted apologies, Tony finally and sincerely asked me to forgive him for the hurt he had caused. As I had done all along, I owned my share of responsibility for our unhappiness and gratefully, and gracefully, forgave him his trespasses.

Chapter Twelve
Secrets & Lies

"The more you take responsibility for your past and present, the more you are able to create the future you seek."
—Celestine Chua

Along with the heart-opening practice of LovingKindness, I believe another significant factor allowed our relationship to unfold in the compassionate, heartfelt and natural way that it did.

As I mentioned earlier, rather than simply blame him, I had to take responsibility for the role I had played in our undoing. Just as he was liable for the choices he made, I had to assume ownership of my own.

What was my part? I have to say it happened largely during the later years of our marriage; times when he came home late from the office; when I waited for hours beyond his normal return home. I had made his dinner, and like a good wife, tried to keep it warm. I worried. I called his office and got no answer. This was before cell phones, so I had no other phone number. There were times I thought about calling the police to see if he had been involved in an accident.

He always apologized and said that he'd been in a meeting with another therapist. Meetings that he had simply forgotten to mention. Meetings that started after his already late office hours. Meetings, I realize now, that were likely with her or other lovers. I believed him, then, but began to feel afraid. Afraid that we were drifting apart. I felt lonely in our marriage. But I didn't say anything for fear that if I told him the truth he would leave. I simply swallowed my feelings and never let on that I was unhappy or afraid for us. I kept my feelings hidden. Secret.

It turns out that we both had secrets; secrets that, like all secrets, wear down the love around us as wind and rain wear down mountains. We kept our secrets for fear of retribution, of becoming vulnerable; afraid that telling the truth might change our lives. And in that very process, our lives were changed; made less than they might have been.

There is a part of me that now understands that there are no mistakes; nothing that isn't perfect, just as it is. Not necessarily pretty and certainly not idyllic, my life has become one of greater acceptance, of not rejecting what is, or at the least, being honest with myself about when I am resisting, and letting it go. Isn't that what our experiences are meant to teach us?

Everything that happens to us, whether we are able to accept it in the moment or not, takes us one more step along our journey. If we are willing to step out of our role as victim and take the time to reflect, I think that we would agree that those things that have happened, if we've been willing to take responsibility for them, have helped us learn and grow.

I doubt that I would be living the life I am living now if Tony and I were still together. It might be better; it might not. All I know is that I have grown incredibly. I have grown spiritually. I've had so many amazing experiences and met so many incredible people in far flung parts of the world that I might otherwise have never known. This isn't justification; it's what I feel is true. I don't have a crystal ball into the past to see how things might have been; all I know is that the pain and the pleasure in my life are now, and always have been, the lifeblood of my future.

If we are willing to learn from them, our experiences can inform our choices as well as increase our capacity to discover what is true, both about ourselves and the world in which we live—the world we create with our thoughts and our choices.

But back to my story.

Ironically, Tony was the one who had told me about the potentially damaging effects of secrets.

I had known for years that there was a secret in my family; something that was so painful for my mother that if I asked her about her life in England or her family, she would become either hysterical or furious. Whether I asked innocently, simply wanting to know about my roots or out of anger that she was keeping half my ancestry and my family from me, she refused to answer. Instead, she would get upset and yell at me or break down in tears, telling me what a horrible daughter I was. My questions seemed to torture her. She refused to say anything about my grandparents or her sister and two brothers. I only knew that they existed because my father had mentioned them.

My parents were married in October 1943, in London, England, one and a half years before the end of World War II. They met at a USO dance and were married with a gang of their Army buddies in attendance. I know this only because of the re-colored post-wedding photo that hung on the wall in the family room of their home after they retired to Florida. I always wondered why her parents weren't there, but knew that asking about their wherabouts would get me nowhere.

Based on snippets of conversation we had had, I knew that my mother was a telephone operator in the WACs (England's Women's Air Corp) during the war. Because of the bombs dropping on London, pregnant service women were sent to safe towns and villages away from the city as their time to deliver neared. Thanks to this policy, I was born in St. Albans, England, a charming little village 19 miles north of London; a place I visited in the early 80's. When I was three or four months old, my U.S. Military Policeman father was shipped with his unit to Paris. Shortly after his departure, my mother and I boarded a ship bound for the U.S., to live with my father's parents and his sister, Muriel, until Dad returned from service.

Along with her sweet little dark-haired bundle of joy, my mother brought something with her that no one, other than my father, was to know. It was a secret I would learn only after her death—and only after holding my father hostage.

Slightly overweight by today's standards, my mother went from one diet to another, from one bottle of pills and one doctor to another. She turned to doctors for every little ailment, assuming that the next physician she saw would have the magic pill that would return her to health.

Happy memories I have of her are few and vague, captured in several photos of her, smiling and holding my little brother, with me standing alongside. In one she is holding my hand. There are others, too; pictures of her enjoying herself during one of the many '31' card games our extended family liked to play. She was a different person, more relaxed and fun in public, than at home.

Other memories are more painful. In my minds' eye, I see her doting on my brother, who was born when I was eight. You would have been forgiven for thinking that the King of England had been born in our house. Mother and Dad were proud of their curly-haired, blond, blue-eyed son; the one who would carry on the family name. When my uncles came over to play cards and drink Boilermakers, my brother received all their attention. Everyone loved him. I had, with his arrival, become invisible.

My brother got everything new while I received hand-me-downs. The new stereo went to him; I got our parent's old one. He went to college for all the right reasons, while I was encouraged to go for my MRS. Perhaps it had more to do with the conditioning of my parent's generation or our family's financial situation, but as the older sister, I resented all the attention and new things my brother received. This went on even into our adult years. It's strange how we mostly remember the experiences that hurt us.

Others in the family were aware of her favoritism and told me later that she didn't seem to like me much. Perhaps my rebellious nature grew out of her attempts to control me. Unlike my brother who was a much easier child than I and always did as he was told, I fought for my own choices, for my right to think in ways that were natural to me and generally contrary to hers. I didn't walk the line my mother had laid out for me and I think she deeply resented my independence.

In that way, I see how her attitude and behavior toward me have influenced my life. Just like the bumper sticker says, I have always questioned authority and sought a truth that felt authentic.

As a Family Therapist, my husband understood the potentially negative impact of family secrets and thought it important for me to learn the secret my mother held so closely. With his encouragement, I made uncovering THE secret my mission.

After my parents retired to Florida, Dad and I fell into what became an unspoken but time-honored tradition—one that would eventually lead to my learning the secret. Within a day or so of my arrival at their home, Dad and I would go for a drive in the countryside, just to talk and catch up with each other. This was our special time together; an opportunity for us to discuss things that mattered to us both; things that my mother never seemed interested in, or was actively resistant to, talking about. He wanted to know about my life and how it was going, financially and personally. Mother seemed to accept these outings as a sacred part of our father-daughter bond and never asked to ride along. The closest my mother and I ever came to this kind of sharing was to go shopping together. Unfortunately, we rarely spoke about anything other than what I considered superficial topics; who had gotten married, divorced, the latest fashions, hairstyles, and so on.

During one of the drives with my dad, I asked him if he knew Mother's secret. When he acknowledged that he did, I asked if he would share it with me if she died before he did. Since there was no life-threatening illness that we were aware of then, along with the knowledge that women typically live longer than men, he said yes.

Several years later, we would find ourselves facing a moment that neither of us would ever forget.

My mother died just after her 81st birthday of a combination of multiple myeloma (bone cancer) and Parkinson's Disease. Mother refused to talk about death, even when she knew hers was imminent. Because of her denial, Dad had to make all the decisions. One that he made revealed to me how much he truly loved her. Perhaps it was simply their generational conditioning, but I recall few public displays of affection between my parents, even at home, as I was growing up.

The decision that revealed the depth of his love involved how to deal with her body. He decided that having her body cremated (she refused to talk about this, too) and scattering her ashes in the Atlantic Ocean, because he knew she loved the sea, was a fitting way for us to say goodbye to her. He coordinated dates with me, my brother and his family, and chartered a fishing boat for the occasion. I flew in from Ohio and my brother, sister-in-law and their two children came in from Illinois.

A burial at sea followed by a fishing expedition seemed a bizarre arrangement, but Dad always did have a somewhat strange sense of practicality. As an adolescent during the Great Depression of 1929, he had learned to never waste anything. One might say that at times he took this to extremes. I vividly recall the 'recycled' sandals he wore. Once, while vacationing at our parent's home, my brother's flip-flops had come apart at the toe piece and he had tossed them in the trash. My father retrieved them and threaded them back together with something that looked like telephone wire. He wore those sandals until the soles finally grew so thin that he was, for all practical purposes, walking barefoot.

Their Florida home was filled with signs of my fathers' frugality. From the homemade 'hooks' he created from 4" nails pounded into a painted piece of wood in the guest bedroom to the do-it-yourself wiring that had switches attached to lights in places that even with a schematic no one could figure out, Dad was the ultimate 'DIYer.'

At the same time, he spared no expense in giving our mother what he felt was a fitting send-off. The day of Mom's Memorial dawned sunny and warm as we packed Dad's coolers with beer, soda, water, turkey sandwiches, and peanut butter & jelly sandwiches (for me, the vegetarian in the family).

I had bought a bouquet of 10 long-stemmed red roses the day before, and Dad had Mom's ashes. Several miles out from shore, our ship's captain dropped anchor so that we could hold our ceremony. We moved to the rear of the boat and Dad reverently opened the bag that held Mom's ashes, tipped it ever so gently and delivered all that was left of her body into the sea. As the waves received her ashes, he simply thanked her for the family now gathered around him and the life that they had shared. Following his lead, we each murmured our gratitude to Mom, and tossed our roses into the deep, greenish waters of the Atlantic. We shared a brief moment of silence as her roses and ashes floated away. My last memory of this most sacred moment is simply that: long stemmed red roses and my mother's ashes bobbing on the water, floating toward the horizon.

With a nod from my father, the ship's captain revved up the motor and steered our boat into deeper waters. Fishing poles, beer and sodas magically appeared. At the end of the day, we had a remarkable catch; one that caused others on the docks when we came back to shore to 'ooh' and 'aah' over. We memorialized our catch forever on Kodachrome and its proof later hung on the photo wall of my father's family room.

Several months later, I visited my father again. It was during this visit that I would hold my father hostage, and finally learn the secret.

Knowing that Dad would just walk away if I asked him to tell me Mother's secret at home, I took him to dinner at one of his favorite seafood restaurants on A1A, the 2-lane highway that hugs Florida's Atlantic coast. Midway between our meal and dessert, I brought up the subject of Mother's secret and asked him to share it with me. All these years later, I still remember that conversation.

Sensing his resistance, I reminded him that he had promised to tell me her secret if she died before he did. Still unwilling, he asked, "Did you get it in writing?" Sitting next to him at the table, I felt a flash of anger, but with the Goddess of reason whispering in my ear, I responded gently, saying, "I didn't think I'd have to." I loved and respected my father and knew him as a man of his word, a man of honor and dignity. Without my conscious intention, those simple words, spoken without anger or upset, allowed him no wiggle room. His honor was now at stake.

But he had another card up his sleeve. Before he would tell me what he knew, he exacted a promise from me: a promise that I had to make if I was to learn the secret. He asked me to promise not to tell my brother. Although time would dictate that recall can lie, there are just some statements that are burned into my memory. This is one of those. As I reluctantly agreed to his grand bargain, he shook his head and said, "I feel like I'm betraying her. Your mother was a Russian Jew."

Knock me over with a feather. To be perfectly honest, his words knocked the wind out of me. I had imagined that it was shame or anger that made Mom keep her secret; maybe she was pregnant with me or that my father wasn't my father. But I wasn't prepared for this!

I've had Jewish friends my entire life—from my late teens all the way to the present—yet my first thought was more a feeling; an unexplicable feeling of heaviness and dread. *Oh, no*, I thought, *What will my friends say?* As my composure returned, that feeling was replaced by a tremendous sense of loss; the loss of a culturally rich heritage. I asked him, then, "But why was that such a secret?" Dad said, "She didn't want you and your brother to suffer." I realized later that, in spite of what I thought she felt about me, she had made a choice to protect us; a choice that she must have thought was an expression of love. Or fear. I didn't then, and I still don't know now, what she might have experienced to create that fear.

As we drove along A1A, back to Dad's one-story sand-colored bungalow so typical of homes in Florida, flashes of insight punctuated the silence. I recalled things she had reacted to, like the 4th of July weekend when two Italian girlfriends and I traveled to Saugatuck, Michigan—a then-favorite waterfront city where college students came to party over the holidays—and pretended to be college-bound Jewish girls from New York. Afterward, my father warned me not to wear the Star of David I had purchased for our weekend get-away. Not appreciating the serious nature of his warning, I continued to wear it, and said nothing when it suddenly disappeared.

I wondered, too, how my mother must have felt about my friendships with Barbara and Sylvia, two Jewish girls I'd met and befriended at my first job. How must she have felt, I wondered, when I enthusiastically relayed my experience of their High Holy Days, their Sabbath rituals and the food my friend's parents so joyfully shared with me. I regaled her with my discovery and love of both sweet and salty Kugel and their sacred rituals, the lighting of the Shabbat candles, their prayers, all things Jewish that I had learned as a seeming 'outsider'.

My synapses fired with recall after recall, each flash of insight creating one intense ah ha! after another. "Oh, now that makes sense," I said. "And that. And that." Dad eventually got tired of my outbursts and said he didn't want to talk about it anymore. I remembered what he'd said about feeling as if he was betraying her, and so, out of respect for his feelings, I tamped down my enthusiasm and joined him in the solemnity of the moment.

After learning the secret, I wondered if the multiple myeloma, the cancer in her bones, might have been a consequence of holding that secret. Given the work I do as an EFT practitioner and Health Coach, I know the effect that our beliefs—about ourselves and others—as well as traumas and negative experiences, can have on our physical health.

How does one cope with hiding their identity; denying their heritage? (As Jews have always done?) Since cancer is a disease that eats away at its host, I wondered if the pain of keeping her birthright a secret might not have literally eaten away at her bones—her body's very structure.

The view that keeping secrets can have devastating effects is supported by several therapists whose work I recently found online. Anita E. Kelly, a doctor of psychology at the University of Notre Dame has studied and written a lot about secrets. While she hasn't found a direct link between keeping secrets and being physically sick, she and researchers did find that those who withhold a lot or are "self-concealers" do show anxiety, depression, and overall body aches and pains... My mother lived with all of those conditions. To sum up Kelly and her team's findings: "Quite simply... secretive people also tend to be sick people... I don't think it's much of a stretch to say that being secretive could be linked to being symptomatic at a biological level."

In the 1970s, James Pennebraker, a psychologist from the University of Texas, also found that "people hiding traumatic secrets showed more incidents of hypertension, influenza, even cancer..."

And now I, too, have a secret. A secret that must be told only now, before the publication of this memoir. Over the years I've wondered how I would tell my brother, knowing that it had to be a necessary sharing, not out of anger or spite, or any wish to hurt him.

As it turns out, my mother held another secret; one I doubt that she was consciously aware of. A month or so after her passing, I was walking along a country road near the horse stables not far from my apartment. I don't recall what I might have been thinking, but as I walked, I had the sense that my mother was communicating with me. There were no flashes of light, no chanting Tibetan monks this time; what I received was an apology. I heard her clearly say that she was sorry, that she loved me and always had, and that all during our relationship she was simply upholding her end of our contract.

Although I was surprised to receive her disembodied message, I understood what she meant about our contract. Years before, I had read a book, *Sacred Contracts*, by Carolyn Myss (mace), a well-known author, medical intuitive and energy healer. In this book, Carolyn describes the agreements, or contracts, that we make at the soul level with respect to our lives; our work, and our relationships. Since there are no mistakes, I believe my mother played her role perfectly in terms of lessons we both had to learn.

Myss offers this metaphor to help us understand how sacred contracts work: before we incarnate, we negotiate a contract with a team of 'masters' and guardians to set up the circumstances of our life. At this heavenly level, we and the masters decide on the life lesson(s) we are to learn to develop our souls and set up our life circumstances accordingly. The only problem is that before we take form in our next life, we must swim through the "river of forgetting". Thus, when we meet our team members, we don't recognize them; they become the greatest challenges, and the greatest teachers, in our life.

Chapter Thirteen

The Lies We Tell Ourselves

"The sun shall always rise upon a new day and there shall always be a rose garden within me. Yes, there is a part of me that is broken, but my broken soil gives way to my wild roses."

–C. JoyBell

I once asked Tony if he was having an affair. It was a playful sort of question, one that arose out of a conversation we were having about a mutual friend to whom I was attracted. We were in the kitchen, cleaning up the dishes after breakfast, following a lovely evening with this friend and I acknowledged that I found him desirable. As Tony and I talked about our friends' charming ways, we touched on the topic of affairs. When I asked him if would ever have an affair, he said, "No, I would never hurt you like that." And, of course, I believed him.

There were other things, too; things that neither of us ever admitted to the other. As close as I thought our relationship was, there was, I learned later, a growing sense of resentment on his part. My fear of losing him, a fear I felt but never told him about caused me to make demands and decisions that I thought would keep him close. I remember his desire to go off by himself for a week, to retreat at a friends' cabin in the hills of Southeast Ohio. When he suggested the idea, I said no, I didn't want him to go. I couldn't imagine being away from him for that long, and selfishly asked him to stay home with me. I thought only of myself.

I know now that I believed my fear; I identified my fear and anxiety as messages that speaking up—telling the truth—would backfire on me. I actually believed that they were there, acting on my behalf, keeping me safe... warning me of the dangers of moving beyond them. From the standpoint of the ego, this is true.

The ego mind, the 'I' thought that is created when we take our body and our mind to be real, to be who we are, is the one that wants us to believe in our fear so that we remain small, out of sight, safe.

As the Buddha said long ago, "We are what we think. All that we perceive begins with our thoughts." Around the age of four or so, we begin to think of ourselves as our bodies and identify with a name that goes with the body we have. Prior to that, we are still close to—still remember ourselves as—simple Beingness; not identified with our bodies as who or what we are. Whether we are judged good or bad, worthy or unworthy, loveable or unloveable, we begin to think of ourselves in keeping with what others say. Or at least what they say about our body; its size, its appearance, its beauty or lack thereof and its behavior, as well as our mind and its behavior.

It turns out that there really are no problems in our lives, unless we see situations and conditions as problems, as limiting factors. From the perspective of the mind—the ego mind—anything or anyone that threatens its sovereignty, its need to be in control or to be right, its right to exist as an entity separate from everyone else, creates a problem. That problem, situation or person becomes something to overcome, deny or avoid.

And that's the problem. The search for inner freedom, for what we've come to call peace of mind, is just that; the search for freedom from the activities and vagaries of the mind. The ego mind, with all its mental gymnastics and identification with the physical body has convinced us of its reality; a reality that when investigated has no legs. No arms. No form. There's nothing there but a seeming form and the belief that that form is me. Inquire into either one of them, and there's nothing and no one there!

If you were to stop right now and try to find your mind, where would you look? What if what we call mind is simply a jumble of some 50,000-70,000 thoughts that pass through our awareness every day? Do they have any solid reality or are they simply like clouds passing over the sun?

Although there's a part of me, the ego, of course, that would like you to think that I came to this realization on my own, that wouldn't be the truth. I had help. Lots of it. So let me tell you that story now.

I stayed in the village after our divorce and eventually bought a wonderful two-story home a block away from the downtown area. Well, in reality, I bought half a house; a 100-year old home that had been converted into a duplex long before I came to town. A friend/co-worker and I both wanted to have our own places to live, so we bought the house together. We shared the mortgage, the front porch and the backyard, but otherwise lived independent of each other.

I loved living there and having a space to call my own. It was a friendly old house with irreplaceable yellow pine floors whose beauty had been hidden under blackened turpentine and an unappealing dark gray carpet. Before moving in, I had the carpet removed and the floors refinished. A lovely arch separated the living and dining rooms and a built-in corner cupboard in the dining room housed some of my trinkets and treasures. I love the little nooks and crannies that so many older homes have and this place had its share. While the house wasn't fancy, after several coats of paint, new windows and those shiny, newly refinished floors, it felt warm and inviting. I loved having friends in for dinner and tea and felt truly happy and safe in my little nest.

A block away from the Dharma Center, my new home had what realtors call the perfect location. There wasn't much that wasn't within walking distance and bicycling was easy and safe on the neighborhood streets. With just one lane of traffic in either direction in the tree-lined downtown business district and cars parked on both sides of the street, I rode my thin-tired road bike down the center of the lane, and with the wind in my hair, felt free and indestructible. While fellow-villagers willingly indulged this kind of behavior, I doubt that drivers passing through town were charmed by our laissez-faire attitude. Living in a community populated by artists, students, poets and dreamers, we were rarely in a rush.

As much as I loved life in what felt like a little piece of Northern California in the midlands of conservative Ohio, I found it challenging to make the kind of living that I wanted. I had been the village's Administrative Assistant for several years, and was now operating a small graphic design/office organizing business. I wanted to do something different, something that would be more meaningful and allow me the freedom to maintain a free and open lifestyle.

Aware of the burgeoning problem of obesity in our culture and with an already formed perspective on healthy eating, gained when I started eating a vegetarian diet, I began to explore possibilities in the field of nutrition. I found an online program offering a degree in holistic nutrition and signed up for it. Next, I had to figure out how to devote myself fully to this program and still support myself. As these things seem to unfold for me, another insight followed on the heels of this question. I called Swamiji in Pennsylvania and asked if I could stay there while I underwent my nutrition studies. His answer was, "Yes, of course. This is your home." And it was my home. My spiritual home.

And so, I went. I sold my half of the house to my next-door-neighbor-mortgage partner, and after fond farewells, brunches, lunches, and a potluck dinner and estate sale with about 20 friends, began the 530 mile trek to Arsha Vidya Gurukulam (AVG) in Saylorsburg, Pennsylvania. Although it was a typically cloudy day when I left the Wellspring, my spirits were high. They grew even higher as I drove onto Interstate 70 East and into a sunny, blue-sky's the limit kind of day!

Although none of us can foresee our future, in retrospect, I see how perfectly the Universe had planned my journey.

I loved living at the ashram again. A few of my gurubhai were still there, working as staff members. The temple priests, their wives, and others I had met and worked with pre-Tony were still there, and in many ways it was, as Swamiji had said, like coming home. While my main focus was my nutrition studies, I helped where I could, both in the kitchen and the office.

After the three-year Vedanta course ended and all the students had left, the ashram had expanded its programs to include cultural events as well as serving as a venue for programs affiliated with Hindu culture. These programs included yoga, Vedic astrology (Jyotish), and Ayurveda.

One day while a Jyotish program was being held at the ashram, I met another Western woman walking on one of the paths. Accustomed as I was to being surrounded by so many India-born residents and visitors to the ashram, meeting another Westerner was a welcome experience. As if we both recognized this, we stopped and began to talk. She told me that she was a nurse and knew Reiki, an energy healing method that I also practiced. As our conversation continued, she asked if I had ever heard about EFT, Emotional Freedom Techniques (now known as Tapping). It was, she said an extremely effective energy healing modality and shared with me her experience of using it with patients who were experiencing pain or anxiety. She also suggested that as a healer I might want to look into it.

And for some reason, I did. I was intrigued by the anecdotal stories I read online of how EFT could heal physical, mental and emotional problems. Thanks to ashram friends who let me practice on them for a variety of issues—from neck pain to emotional wounds—I discovered that EFT truly worked, and that I had a natural affinity for using it.

I also recognized the power these techniques held for clearing the kinds of traumatic and painful experiences that so often drive emotional eating. I thought EFT might just hold the secret to helping people lose weight once their avoidance tactics and unhealthy behaviors around food and other addictive substances were eliminated.

I was on fire. It suddenly seemed as if my spiritual journey was unfolding into my worldly work. I could now engage in work that I loved; work that would allow me to contribute to the transformation of other's lives, and earn the kind of money I had hoped for. That nurse who told me about EFT? I never saw her again. Who was she and why did she cross my path at that particular moment? Was she another of my 'middle angels,' pointing me in the direction I needed to go next? And why did I go to my computer immediately to learn about EFT? These are the hidden 'coincidences' that occur in our lives. Deepak Chopra calls these seeming coincidences and experiences 'synchrodestiny.'

Synchronicity and destiny; the integration of time and space that we often call coincidence deserves our attention—and our willingness to listen, to follow the lead, and the leaning. Taking the time to become conscious of these 'out-of-the-blue' connections is so much more essential than most of us realize. I love noticing, in retrospect, how these seemingly co-incidents and experiences have always led to the next 'right' step on my journey.

They also require trust; trust that the Universe, God, Great Spirit, Allah or whatever you call that Something Greater than yourself, wants only what is best for us. What's best for us doesn't always come wrapped up with a sweet little red bow, but, rather with a life lesson or opportunity to grow—even in those moments when we might wish for something different.

So much of my life has been based on an intrinsic understanding of the importance of trust. To some degree, I have always been a risk-taker, an adventurer; curious and always ready to step outside the box my family or my culture had created for me and simply follow my own leanings. I knew in my heart that the Universe would always take care of me. All I needed to do was listen, surrender and let it take me where it would. This was a necessary, although not always easy, choice.

After completing my nutrition program, it was time to leave the ashram and take this work out into the world. But where should I go? As much as I loved Wellspring, I didn't think the conservative population in the cities surrounding the village would be open-minded enough to explore energy medicine: the field EFT and other energy healing modalities have been dubbed. And I felt complete with Wellspring. I had learned what I was there to learn and it was time for a new place, new people, and another new beginning.

As the Universe would have it, a fellow student of Swamiji's with whom I had studied in the Northern California course, was living in Durham, North Carolina. She was working as a nurse at UNC-Chapel Hill, and told me that the Durham-Chapel Hill area seemed like a fairly liberal place and that I might find an open-minded population in North Carolina's Research Triangle.

Little did I know how true that would be. I moved to Chapel Hill and created a small practice there... while the Universe continued slowly unfolding its intentions for me.

My second prayer—not quite as intense as the gut-wrenching, down-on-my-knees prayer that had originally taken me to the teachings of the East, but heart-felt and sincere, nonetheless—came after I'd been living in North Carolina for two years.

I was visiting Swamiji's ashram in Pennsylvania, attending the wedding of a young woman I had grown close to while I was there on staff. We had stayed in touch after Tony and I married and left the ashram. I was delighted by the invitation to witness her marriage to a lovely Indian man who also attended the retreat programs there.

I stayed on at the ashram for a couple of days after the wedding, hanging out with Swamiji and relaxing in the peace and quiet there. The morning of the day I was to leave, I walked into the lecture/meditation hall and over to the small temple on the right side of the hall. Seated inside the temple in all his beautiful, shining, black glory is a large statue of Daksinamurthy. This murthy or form represents Lord Siva as the first guru (teacher) or Daksina, the one who sees the Universal Truth. In India he is considered the God of Wisdom.

I've always loved this particular form and the ritual that surrounds his presence. Every morning at 5:30 a.m., one of the two temple priests at the ashram lovingly washes this 5' tall statue with milk, buttermilk, honey, water and liquefied sandalwood paste. No one else was in the meditation hall/temple when I walked in about 10 a.m., but the large, wooden doors with beautifully carved lotus flowers were 'coincidentally' still open. They were usually closed by 9 a.m.

Although I had planned to simply pay my respects to the ashram deity, as I knelt before Daksinamurthy my unhappiness spilled out, along with the admission that the knowledge I had gained wasn't working for me. I wasn't living the life I had imagined the study of Vedanta offered, and I needed help.

Surrendering. Again. Giving it all up and telling the truth. Even to a stone statue that represents a Hindu God. I realize now that it doesn't really matter who or what we pray to. As long as we do it. As long as we acknowledge that we don't know; that we allow ourselves to admit the struggle, the pain and suffering and simply surrender. To let the truth of our experience rise up from the heart.

Perhaps it's simply about letting the ego fall away for a moment; the ego that thinks it needs to be strong and independent to be safe. The ego keeps us separate when what we really want is connection; when all we want is to know that we are loved and cared for. Prayer makes us vulnerable, or perhaps more correctly, acknowledges our inherent vulnerability, our powerlessness in the face of life's vagaries.

In an odd sort of way, I love that feeling of powerlessness. Of recognizing, perhaps, that I really know nothing. My only job here on this planet is to feel what I'm feeling, tell the truth about it, and to ask. For guidance. For help. For direction on the journey. Without knowing from where or when it will come— only to trust that it will.

As the Dalai Lama says, "In the final analysis, the hope of every person is simply peace of mind."

Chapter Fourteen
There Are No Accidents!

"All you have to do is witness the disappearance of a single thought. Stay there with open attention and witness the space that is left."
—Gilbert Schultz.

It is comforting to know that even if we're not 'religious,' there is someone or something that hears our heartfelt prayers. Once again, within two weeks, I knew that this prayer, too, had been heard. Stone statue or not, after praying at the feet of Daksinamurthy, I heard from a stranger (another middle angel) about a meditation center on the outskirts of a small city in the middle of North Carolina; a town that is the epitome of what is known in the south as the Bible Belt.

It was clearly one of those 'synchro-destiny' experiences Deepak Chopra writes about. I was looking for a new apartment in Carrboro, North Carolina, a small liberal community attached at the hip to Chapel Hill. I've always been attracted to college towns, and although Carrboro doesn't have a college, its proximity to Chapel Hill and UNC lends it that same appeal. I had arranged to meet a guy named Bill so that I could view an apartment in a large, older home just blocks from Weaver Street Market (WSM), a food co-op and gathering place that is the hub of Carrboro's downtown. Wooden picnic tables and small metal tables carpet the lawn area in front of WSM, creating a friendly alliance among diners, writers and others with their laptops, or folks simply meeting friends.

Bill told me that the house I was there to see belonged to friends of his and he was showing it to me as a favor to them. At the end of the house tour, he asked to know a little about me.

After telling him the basics—name, current work and where I lived—I followed it up with an atypical response. Rather cheekily, I said, "Tell me about you. What do *you* do?"

He told me briefly about his work and then said, '... and I'm a student of Advaita Vedanta.' *Whoa, I said to myself! What?* "I'm a student of Advaita Vedanta," I responded, thinking *no one ever introduces themselves like this. After all, how many people have even heard of Advaita Vedanta?*

Immediately curious, I asked, 'Who is your teacher?,' realizing at once that this meeting just might be about more than a new place to live! As we sat on the wooden bench inside the entryway, he began to tell me his story; a story that inspired and intrigued me—and made me hungry for what he had. What did he have? A profound sense of peace and contentment came over him as he spoke about his teacher and his own awakening: an awakening that called to my heart and my own deep longing.

I needed to know more. It turns out that he had met his teacher, V. Ganesan, the grandnephew of Ramana Maharshi, at a small meditation center just outside of Asheboro, North Carolina. All I knew about Asheboro besides its reputation as the buckle of the Bible Belt, was that it is also the home of the North Carolina Zoo. Friends had taken me to the Zoo shortly after I arrived in North Carolina but I hadn't set foot in Asheboro since. As part of my studies with Swami Dayananda, I had heard of Ramana Maharshi, a revered Indian sage, whose teachings we had studied through several small books written about him.

As Bill tripped out on what had happened during his meetings with V. Ganesan, I felt both joy and envy. I wanted to know what he knew, to experience the same kind of happiness, and to feel as alive and as blissful as he, as he shared with me how his life had been transformed by the teaching of Self-Inquiry as taught at this meditation center.

I wanted to know more, of course, about the meditation center and how I might meet V. Ganesan. Bill told me the name of the place was AHAM, which surprised me as Aham is the Sanskrit word for 'I' or 'I Am'. As I would learn later, AHAM, all capital letters, is, according to this meditation center, an acronym for The Association of Happiness for All Mankind.

As soon as I left Bill, I called Maria, a woman I had met shortly after my move to Chapel Hill. We had become fast friends, sharing similar values and perspectives regarding both environmental issues and spirituality. She was a dedicated follower of Eckhart Tolle and several other contemporary teachers, and had a small retreat center on the edge of Chapel Hill where she showed spiritually-based videos. In spite of living in Chapel Hill for the past 30 or so years, she had never heard of AHAM.

I became a woman on a mission. I first went to the Internet to find AHAM's website. From there I found their phone number and called the center. The woman who answered the phone told me that while there weren't any programs or retreats currently in progress, we were welcome to visit. More than that, she invited us to join them for lunch one day.

And so, we did. Within about a week of receiving that invitation, Maria and I drove the hour or so to Asheboro and onto the meditation center property. The first thing I saw as we drove up the driveway was an unassuming brick ranch-style house on the left, at the top of the hill, along with several small buildings and a couple of trailers on our right. Seeing the trailers, Maria and I looked at each other somewhat skeptically, but since we were already there, decided to go in and see what this place was about. The trailers wouldn't be the only surprise that day held.

As we walked up several steps and into the foyer, we were welcomed by several people who introduced themselves as staff members. They looked pretty normal and were certainly friendly. One of them was Gertrude, a Dutch woman whose presence would prove beneficial for my Dutch friend Maria's comfort level.

Leaving our shoes on one of the tall silver wire racks in the foyer, we stepped into a medium-sized kitchen that held, along with your typical kitchen stove and counter, three refrigerators. This, we were told, was where both the daily and program (retreat) meals were prepared. Just beyond the kitchen sink and counter was the dining area with a long table and chairs enough for ten or so people.

Soon after we were seated, a tall, pear-shaped man with small blue tattoos on his arms entered the dining area. He was A. Ramana, the co-founder of AHAM. Although I wasn't aware that I had gone there with any preconceived notions of what we might find, it didn't take long for my previously unseen notions to present themselves. Having studied with Swami Dayananda, a traditional teacher who looked, spoke and acted the part in every way, this man, Ramana, appeared to be the polar opposite of the tradition in which I had been steeped.

I was shocked by his physical appearance. He was a large man; his pear shaped body and tattooed arms were the first characteristics that shattered my illusion of what a spiritual teacher 'should' look and sound like. Born in Texas, he had a slight southern accent. And so the picture is complete; my initial impression and disrespectful description of his physical form was that he was a 'tall, fat, tattooed Texan.'

We shared a simple, yet delicious vegetarian lunch of cheese enchiladas, guacamole, chips and tea with him and six or seven staff members. Throughout the meal, and for several hours following it, Maria and I peppered Ramana with questions. He told us about his childhood experience of awakening and how he came to co-found AHAM, based on a later, more permanent awakening.

My skepticism of his role as a spiritual teacher colored my questions. Rather than being open and available to learn what he was there to share, I was totally caught in my ego. Many of my questions were not-so-subtle attempts at validating my experience and my studies with Swamiji. I wish I could say that I had been more curious and honoring of A. Ramana and his experience. To this day, I regret that I behaved so arrogantly during our first meeting.

Regret aside, that is the truth of how I came to AHAM and to this Ramana. And, I am grateful to say that, in spite of my arrogance, he treated me with grace and compassion. I'm not justifying my arrogance, but perhaps as a result of my attitude, I received a teaching that day, a simple, yet powerful instruction that he shared with me, despite or perhaps because of, my behavior. He proved himself wiser when he looked straight at me and said, *"You know, there's a big difference between knowing and knowing about."*

Bingo. Busted. I knew then that he had me. I knew *about* the Self. I also knew that until I knew it *as* myself, I really knew nothing worthwhile.

Sitting at the dining table next to Ramana, I was humbled by his words. I felt a shift. My mind grew silent. This stranger knew me better than I knew myself. And I wanted, no, I needed to know what he knew. I wanted that knowing more than life itself. My heartbreak and longing for this truth had put me on the journey and now it had brought me here—to this very table in a little known meditation center, next to a fat, tattooed, yet wise Texan in the Bible Belt of North Carolina. Strange as this scene might have been, I knew that none of this was accidental.

I'm reminded of a story from Chandogya Upanishad, a principle text within the Vedas, about a young boy, Shvetaketu, whose father sent him to a teacher to learn about the spiritual life. When he returned home twelve years later, the boy was arrogant, proud of the knowledge he had gained. His father, Uddalaka, noticing that, said to his son: *"You seem to be proud of all this learning, but did you ask your teacher for that spiritual wisdom which enables you to hear the unheard, think the unthought and know the unknown?"*

Their dialogue continues: *"What is that wisdom, Father?"* asked the son.

HEART BREAKING OPEN

Uddalaka said to Shvetaketu:

As by knowing one lump of clay, dear one,
we come to know all things made out of clay:
That they differ only in name and form,
while the stuff of which all are made is clay;
As by knowing one gold nugget, dear one,
we come to know all things made out of gold:
That they differ only in name and form,
while the stuff of which all are made is gold;
As by knowing one tool of iron, dear one,
we come to know all things made out of iron:
that they differ only in name and form,
while the stuff of which, of which all are made is iron
So through that spiritual wisdom, dear one,
We come to know that all of life is one."

CHAPTER FIFTEEN
THE END OF THE SEARCH

"Your outer journey may contain a million steps; your inner journey only has one: the step you are taking right now."
—Eckhart Tolle,
<u>The Power of Now: A Guide to Spiritual Enlightenment</u>

As we drove back to Chapel Hill, Maria and I were still somewhat shocked, skeptical and intrigued by the outward appearance of A. Ramana. His body was the antitheses of what either of us 'thought' a spiritual teacher should look like. And tattoos? Come on! We carried on with our mocking commentary until something in me shifted. I recalled my experience at Ramana's table, and said to Maria, "Enough. Something happened to me back there in Asheboro, and I want whatever wisdom and clarity I might gain from that man."

During our visit, we had learned about the programs offered by AHAM, and I had signed up for their introductory weekend. Within a few weeks I attended that retreat and registered for the next program—their foundational eight-day Intensive Self-Inquiry Training, aka I SIT. Maria was unsure, waiting to hear my impression of these first two programs, before she would participate in their offerings.

I struggle to find words that might clearly express the profound shift I experienced during that I SIT. I remember that at the end of the eight-day training, Elizabeth MacDonald (Young), the Senior Trainer and Co-founder of AHAM, asked the nine of us for whom she had facilitated the program, if we had gotten what we came for. I was stunned by her question because I realized that in spite of having been on this journey for so many years, I wasn't exactly sure what I was looking for—until I found it. Or, it found me.

This experience was like the example so many teachers use of a person searching for their glasses, only to discover that they're where they've been all along; perched on top of their own head. They search and search, looking in, under and at every surface, in every nook and cranny where they could have possibly been dropped or left. We even accuse others of knowing where they are and purposely not telling us. We try to engage them in the search, and if we're really lucky, one of those people will help us by simply pointing them out to us. Right here, closer than close. So close that we couldn't see them. Right where they've been 'hiding' all along!

Discovering the truth of oneself, of Beingness itself, is akin to that. The problem is that we just don't know it. We overlook it and spend much of our lives searching outside ourselves, looking for that perfect relationship, that perfect object or experience that will give us the permanent happiness or contentment we seek. This goes on simply because we take ourselves, the awareness that we are, for granted. We are ignorant of our own presence; our magnificence.

How can this be? This is, in fact, the conundrum that philosophers and scholars have explored and written about for centuries. And once we 'get' it, once we see for ourselves that what we thought we needed to find was never really lost, we strive to 'stay' there. As if we could ever go anywhere else. As if we could ever *lose* ourselves again.

We bask in that knowing... for a while. And then, upon returning to our daily lives, we are challenged to 'operate,' to live, to experience life from this knowing—from this Beingness that we are.

Following the I SIT, I participated in every training and support program in AHAM's curriculum, grateful to be with people who so clearly understood the depth of my longing and could share a process that could put out the fire.

Now that the fire in me had been quenched by the deep recognition of my own Beingness, I was anxious to learn how I could *Be* this Awareness and still live in the world.

When we discover the truth of who we are, we also discover that there is nothing that isn't me, the Self. This is the beauty and the challenge of Self-Knowledge. What do you do, how do you live in a world that is based on separation and ego-based independence when you have seen through that apparent duality into the Oneness of 'everything?'

This process of relearning how to live in the world of appearances, where things seem to be separate and other than you, is called integration. AHAM's curriculum, as well as the teachings of Adyashanti and Eckhart Tolle in particular, help us learn how to live with this knowing while living in the phenomenal world.

The challenge, and the practice that continues to this day, is not just to know myself, but to *be* my Self; the real Self that I am, in spite of the fact that my eyes still see a world of objects that appears before them—as something or someone still 'out there.'

The practice becomes one of seeing not just through our eyes, not experiencing the world through any of our senses, but seeing through the Heart, as the Heart.

Here's what I'm trying to say: We take ourself, our true Self, for granted. The 'job' or The Work, as Byron Katie calls it, is to recognize that behind every experience; behind the eyes that see, the ears that hear, the tongue that tastes, the skin that is touched and the nose that senses fragrance, there is something we call awareness. Thanks to this awareness, we are aware of what we are seeing, hearing, tasting and touching. If we stop and ask the question, "who is aware of those things, those experiences?" we respond naturally with "I am." But what or who is that I? Who is that I that we are so sure of? Who is that I that knows what it knows, but doesn't seem to know itself?

Within that recognition, within that experience, lies the truth behind the seeking and the seeker. Why, if it's that simple, that available, do we not know it? How do we miss it?

According to the ancient Vedic texts, the problem is simply one of ignorance; of missing our true Self and taking the truth of who we really are for granted. We think that we are this body that we 'have.' In spite of the fact that we are also aware of our thoughts, we think that we are the mind that judges and interprets our experiences. Taking ourselves to be the body and the mind, and thinking that the life we have, with all of its joys and sorrows, is all there is, we find ourselves wanting an unendingly elusive 'more.'

Or less. Whenever we try to escape or deny uncomfortable thoughts, rather than just see them as projections of the mind, we give the mind, and its thoughts, more power than they deserve. If I were to ask you now if you *have* a body or you *are* the body, you might feel confused. If I were to ask you now if you *have* a car or you *are* your car, there would be no confusion. From the standpoint of who you really are, both your body and your car are vehicles, forms of transportation, meant to get you from one point to another.

The same logic operates with respect to the mind. Just as we can objectify the body, i.e., see it as clearly as we see any other object, we are also aware of our thoughts. And what is the mind but a bundle of thoughts? Just as the body can be viewed as the vehicle that propels us through the world, the mind and the five senses are the tools through which we experience the world. The problem is that we also take the mind and the thoughts to be who and what we are.

Witness the mind and its thoughts for just a moment. Think of the mind in the same way that you might think of a nosy neighbor; one who tells you all your other neighbor's secrets. Your experience is that she makes up a lot of stuff based on what she thinks she sees. You politely listen to her, taking what she says with a grain of salt, and you move on.

What might happen if you did this with your own thoughts? What if you paid polite attention to your mind and moved on? What if you recognized that the mind is simply a jumble of thoughts, most of which have little to do with improving your life or the world? Would you give it as much credit or power as you do now?

Our mind, like our body-vehicle, is meant to be our servant; the administrative staff—not the boss. Not knowing that we are this Awareness because of which we are aware of the mind and all its thoughts, we give our minds an exalted position; one that it neither deserves nor appreciates. Instead of using the mind, the mind uses us. We are directed by thoughts that often do us a real disservice. Those thoughts sound like this: "I'm bored, let's eat something." "I'm worthless." "I'm not good enough." "I'm the best." "I hate them." "They're losers." "There's something wrong with me."

"What's the one common factor in all of those thoughts?" What must be there before, or behind, the thoughts? What can I say but 'me?" I am there, behind them all. The one who thinks those thoughts, who is aware of them, must be there before the thoughts can be perceived.

If we take a moment to examine a thought, what do we find? Do we discover anything substantial? I'm not a philosopher, and fortunately, it doesn't take a philosopher to know for certain that I am here, aware of each thought, aware of each emotion, just as I am aware of what is happening with the body. You have a thought; you have an emotion or feeling, and you have a body. Who is it that *has* all these 'things?'

This is the teaching of Self-Inquiry: the teaching also known as Self Knowledge. It's the teaching that I studied with Swamiji for all those years—years that were preparing me for AHAM and the Self-Inquiry process that they share. The ultimate question, as proposed by Ramana Maharshi, is 'Who Am I?' Asking that question requires a context, a container and, at least for me, someone pointing out that the Silence and Stillness behind or between the thoughts is the underlying, ever-present truth; the very Self that I have been seeking.

On the way to knowing myself as the one, unchanging awareness, I experienced several different types of meditation; each with a different purpose or end point. Whether we meditate to connect with or tune into our true Self, to live with a greater sense of Presence or simply to relieve stress, meditation allows us to experience a shift whose benefits can be appreciated in many ways, not the least of which is expressed in one of Einsteins' oft-quoted statements, "You can't solve a problem using the same thinking that created it."

This quote makes the distinction between prayer and meditation, and speaks to a necessary mind shift: "Prayer is when you talk to God, meditation is when you listen."

When we begin to meditate, we discover, first, how very busy the mind is; most minds have a hard time being quiet. Once we discover the truth of who we truly are, we don't really need the mind to be quiet. Just as the sun is unaffected by clouds passing across it, we are unaffected by thought. We are the observer; the awareness that witnesses the mind as well as all other objective 'reality.'

When we are focused on a task we need the mind; it is an important tool for functioning in the world. Without the mind, how could we carry out our daily affairs? Isn't that what the mind is for?

The 'problem' with the mind is its outer focus; the mind is all about the world around us, whether that world is limited to the body that transports 'us' from place to place, or the world we perceive beyond the body. The mind, along with our senses, is about the objects that appear before us. They tell us nothing about our inner world, and ignore the awareness or consciousness without which we would not be aware of the world or our thoughts.

When the mind is quiet and the senses unaware of the objects of perception, as in deep sleep, there is only consciousness or awareness. That Presence because of which we can say, "I slept well" is there in its essential state.

This mind and all its projections are seen by this Presence, this conscious essence. With consciousness we can see through the mind and experience the peace and contentment we'd been hoping that all our 'stuff,' our relationships, and our experiences might give us.

We seek escape from the ups and downs. We try to find some constancy; one permanent something we can count on. Something that won't ever change. We look for love, for the peace and contentment that loving and feeling loved gives us—in all the wrong places.

Some of us find our discontent eased by distraction. We drink, we eat, we gamble, we drug, we shop, we love; all in an effort to escape our discomfort. We think that the answer lies outside us; in the next person or the next experience. If I have that car, I will be happy. If I have that job, that house, that lover or that partner, my life will be complete.

And then, if we're lucky (yes, lucky) and lose that relationship or that job, we experience a different kind of grace. Perhaps we discover that we are now free to pursue our true passion, to create something that our fear of stepping into the unknown kept us from.

How many stories have you heard about people who, despairing after losing their job, their livelihood, discover that they now have the freedom to pursue their dreams?

If we are truly fortunate, we also take the inner journey; the journey where the truth of our longing and the truth of our freedom live. We venture into the heart of being; where we can awaken to the truth that *we already are* the peace and happiness we have been seeking. That we are that love and contentment we've been wishing and hoping the world would give us; hoping we could find it as a result of our relationships and acquisition of 'things.'

We have always been that Love. It has always been there. Here. All along. Like the glasses on the head of the person searching for them. Or the keys in your pocket. Just too close to see!

Whatever loss one has experienced, whether it is the death of a beloved person, a pet, our home or our livelihood, our willingness to experience the pain it creates carries with it the potential to open the heart, to break it open; to let us experience the incredible love that abides there. That has always been there. And that love is the love that never dies, that is never lost, that always simply *is*. As long as the heart is, the unconditioned, unchanging love that can never *not* be, is there.

My trajectory began with meditation and is, in fact, recovered there, every time I sit with the intention of meditating. The potential to experience it again and again is there, every time we practice. And every time we experience it, our experience of it expands... until we see that that love—unconditioned, unconditional and pure—is the truth of who we are. This is the truth that is reflected when we love, whether we love another or simply extend that love to the reflection we see in the mirror.

We recognize that nothing in the world can give us the lasting, permanent happiness we seek. For reasons unknown to me, I came to that conclusion relatively early in my life, with just enough loss and struggle to put me on the path toward truth; a truth that once recognized at the deepest level possible, frees us to be whole, to see ourselves as complete and lacking nothing.

The prayerful surrender following the ending of my first marriage, and the role of Metta practice in my second, were ultimately about the willingness to admit that when I take myself to be this body or this mind, I am, ultimately, powerless. I see myself then as a limited, frail human being who wanders the world seeking love, comfort, self-acceptance and some modicum of wisdom.

Rather than a sign of weakness, this capacity to show up and tell the truth about our pain and our yearning requires great strength. It takes courage to admit that we don't know; and this, I believe, is the road we must all take if we are to live the life for which we were born. That life is one of recognition; of re-cognizing the amazing Beingness, the Awareness, the Love that we are.

No longer shackled to the idea that we are small, limited, powerless creatures, we begin to live as God wants us to... living in the Light, as the Light. In Love, as Love. There is nothing more amazing, more humbling, more freeing than to wake up to this truth.

What is most important, once one sees with clarity, is to live from there. The practice of remembering this truth, of continuing to ask, is to see for ourselves that we are so much more than we have taken ourselves to be. We are blessed to gain this knowledge. Blessed to know once and for all, that the power that lights our eyes, that empowers our ears and our imagination is the same power; the power that Jesus reminds us of when he says that each of us has the same capacity that he has, that we, too, will perform miracles. Perhaps our miracles won't be as grand as Christ's, but we'll never know until we surrender; until we give ourselves over to the power that is God.

As our practice, we return to the question, Who Am I, really? When there is identification with thoughts or feelings, when there is identification as a doer, this question is what returns us to clarity, to stillness, to truth, moment to moment.

The truth of what is so now is that while the seeking may be over, the practice—the practice of checking in and seeing where attention is from moment to moment—continues. The practice of stopping. Of being still. Of tuning in to the Present... the ever present Presence that I am.

This is how we stay here, in the very heart of Being. In the Truth of who I AM. I AM. Who and what I, and you, are... and have always been.

With gratitude for the blessings of this life, I AM. Love.

The perspective is different now, of course, but in many ways, that young girl I once was lives on. Her sense of curiosity about the world, her willingness to step into the unknown, and to keep growing, continue even as I grow. Older... Wiser... Open...

To My Reader,

Thank you so much for joining me on this journey into the truth we humans seek. I hope that reading my story has encouraged or affirmed your own journey.

If you loved, or even liked, my story and have a minute or two to spare, I would truly appreciate a brief review on the page or site where you purchased the book.

Reviews from readers like you are one of the best ways to share your experience and help new readers discover the benefits of reading a book like *Heart Breaking Open*.

Thank you so much!

Lina Landess
linalandess.com

ABOUT THE AUTHOR

Lina Landess is the Founder and Practitioner at Truly Healthy You, an Emotion-based Wellness Practice whose primary function is to help clients reclaim their health, from the inside out. A small, but growing number of physicians, mental health professionals and scientists (physicians such as Dr. Gabor Mate, Dr. Bruce Lipton, a Developmental Biologist, and researcher Lynne McTaggart) are recognizing the effect that traumatic experiences, especially Adverse Childhood Experiences (ACE), can have on physical health. Although she came to this work 'late' in life, Lina saw how EFT (Emotional Freedom Techniques) i.e., Tapping, and Matrix Reimprinting (an advanced form of EFT) coupled with her focus on awakening to the truth of who we really are could create a safe, spiritually-based and compassionate container for healing the effects of traumatic experiences for her clients.

Prior to her work as a Wellness Coach, Lina spent many years living and studying with, and assisting spiritual masters in the institutions mentioned in the book. Her worldly experiences as a secretary, a graphic artist and a Silicon Valley recruiter positioned her to play key roles in these centers; roles that included writing and editing source materials, letters and other administrative materials.

Although this is Lina's first book, as the call to Truth and Unconditional Love requires, there very well might be another percolating right now.

To learn more about Lina's offerings of EFT, Matrix Reimprinting, and Mindful Meditation, please visit Lina's website: linalandess.com, where you will also find her blog and other useful information.

www.ingramcontent.com/pod-product-compliance
Lightning Source LLC
Chambersburg PA
CBHW021131300426
44113CB00006B/374